Have you ever wondered about your parents or your adult children: 'What on God's great green earth are they *thinking?!* Boomers and their Millennial children grew up in different Americas and are now trying to understand each other and their quickly evolving world.

Boomers:

Give this book to your kids so they have a better insight into where you are in life.

Millennials:

Give this book to your parents instead of a trinket or a tie.

Fireworks!

A fearless look at the Baby Boomers
in old age and the Millennials they raised.
Profane, witty, irreverent and not for the
faint of heart.

By

LESLIE BAKER

www.bookstandpublishing.com

Published by
Bookstand Publishing
Morgan Hill, CA 95037
4710_3

Cover Photo: Nagatoshi Shimamura on Unsplash

ISBN 978-1-63498-829-2

Printed in the United States of America

TABLE of CONTENTS

INTRODUCTION

I f you're old and anticipating one of those cute, rude, funny little books about how to be your effervescent best at 110 years old, this isn't it. My goal is to illuminate a few potholes in the aging process, not to blow smoke up your pant leg. This also isn't a paean to the Millennial children we Boomers have raised. While many of us have great kids, some of us tried so hard to give our children *everything* that we inadvertently burdened them with a sense of entitlement that has done them no favors.

A lot of us Boomers already have one foot in the grave, so most of the geriatric material (Hospice, incontinence, funerals, you know, all the *fun* stuff) is in the first half of the book. Millennials need to know these things about their parents, but parents don't want to talk about them.

Thirty years ago, a friend and I were having lunch at The Madonna Inn, a garish hotel whose restaurant was known for it's decadent Black Forest cake. I was surprised when Susan skipped a ladylike salad and ordered a huge slab of that cake as her entree. She said something I've sometimes forgotten over the years, but which always comes back to me: "Life is short, eat dessert first." Like so much of aging, there's a return to childhood in eating dessert first, but this one's a much happier regression than most of the others.

Now, you're saying to yourself: "Wait a minute here, I thought this *wasn't* going to be one of those perky damned screeds telling me how rosy old age is!" No, it's not, but I'm just following my friend's credo and giving you the dessert first. That's as good as it gets, you snarky old toot, so press on and eat your vegetables.

For young people, the caveat to indulging in dessert first is that it's important that you've *earned* it, that it's not being covered by a credit card whose balance keeps growing. That way you can revel in it with a clear conscience!

There's an old story about putting a live frog in a pot of cold water: he'll never notice when the pot is slowly brought to a boil and not know he's dying til he's dead.

That frog is pretty much how the author views a large swath of the American populace. Whether they're comfortable and living in la-la-land or hoping to wake up tomorrow and find that all things are free, many are focused on how idyllic socialism (like a toasty jacuzzi) sounds.

Like the frog, we all enjoy our comforts, but there's not much agreement to be found in our country about whether or not we need to *earn* our lifestyles.

Primarily because of technology and the changes it brings daily, the old people and the young people of today have less in common than any of the generations before them. This book attempts to re-introduce them to each other and to encourage them in a dialog about the future of our country, the travails aging parents are facing and a few thoughts on child rearing.

I've long considered writing a book on the challenges of aging. But to whom would you market such a thing? I think this is how some of those clever mini-books that we're given on Birthdays Ending in Zero end up as gag gifts. Someone starts a serious book on aging and then decides that they have to either lighten it up or jump off a bridge.

Basically, *nobody* wants to hear about this getting old crap. A friend recently reminded me that 'old' is your age plus 10 years. Sigh. If you're middle-aged (an ever-changing calculation) and sandwiched between fetching your parents' prescriptions and making it to your kids' soccer games, you're probably running your butt off and don't have time to read *anything*. If you're really young (anything under 40 qualifies) you may feel that old age is a problem that technology will have solved by the time *you* get there. And if you're already old, you're so sick and tired *being* old that reading about it isn't your idea of a good time. But if it's between cleaning your dentures and reading this, I think you'll enjoy this more.

What on earth can a senior write on aging that a young person would bother *reading*, much less take seriously? That it's a depressing, irreversible disintegration of every system in your body and mind? That the incidence of mortifying failures in routine functions becomes the norm? That you're even more aware of it than is your audience, thank you very much? Gee, there's some high entertainment.

As we're sucked into the vortex of old age, many of us are stunned by its cruelty and can feel powerless to convey this shock and helplessness to others. Our contemporaries get it, but those younger, especially our own children, are pretty oblivious. I get that they're busy living their lives and I want them to do exactly that until they can no longer ignore what's going on with Mom and Pop. Some children may be helping with the physical and monetary aspects of *really* aging and unwell parents, but as long as parents put on a show of being 'just fine' the kids have no reason to question that. What are a parent's options? To become a whiny, clinging, complaining dependent? That will come soon enough and there doesn't seem to be a lot of middle ground between that and just trudging through it.

I think that old age is almost harder for someone like me, who's sailed through life with so few physical issues (batshit crazy, but that doesn't *show*) that I just don't have the resiliency to deal with a balky knee, unreliable bladder or failing memory. There are times when I want to take a stick to some faulty body part, whack it and tell it to shape up! Never say never, but at this stage, I refuse to hobble onto that old-folks-merry-go-round of endless doctor's appointments and juggling medications. If it requires something more heavy-duty than aspirin or more invasive than tweezers, my current course of treatment relies on whiskey and water.

One of the ways I've dealt with an unwelcome retirement and too much time on my hands is by writing a folksy column for our local paper. It runs through one editor's tenure and not the next because I'm too political for my own good. Some of those columns are inserted in this book and still titled 'Yesterday's News.' I live in a small mountain town in Arizona, so they're pretty country, as am I.

Another add-on you'll see in most chapters is 'Advice.' All of us seniors are fonts of knowledge we'd like to share. These tidbits are laid out in no relation to their preceding text, so don't be confused by abrupt u-turns in topic when you reach one.

I've always been a nit-picker about ending sentences with prepositions, alternating tense and the like, but you'll have to take off your editor's hat for a while, because my filters have gotten as old and worn out as the rest of me. Choosing among the grammar, the swearing, the attitude and the topics, there's something here to annoy everyone; yell back and enjoy!

...1...ATTITUDE

Lyndon Johnson once said that "Being President is like being a jackass in a hailstorm. There's nothing to do but to stand there and take it." That pretty much sums up being old, too. There *are* those 100 year-olds who decide to get a diploma that eluded them early in life, take a parachute jump or learn a new language and they can be pretty inspirational if you're not the eye-rolling sort.

The rest of us can put on a twinkly face and swoon over the grandchildren; beatifically muse over how blessed a life we've been given; determinedly learn to use each new tech tool or go all perky and tough and sign up for Senior Runs. Most of us have toyed with those roles and others that make us feel that we're not churlish, crabby old buzzards ungrateful for a full life. We don't enjoy old people like that and are pretty sure that no one else does, either.

Playing golf, hiking or keeping active in any number of ways is not only good for your physical well being but certainly improves your outlook on life, too. Sometimes, though, I get the feeling that I've already crossed this bridge.

In the 1990's, a poem about a woman vowing to wear purple when she got old became popular. I'd *always* worn purple (preferably spangled with sequins) and was feeling older than God's wet-nurse right then, so I figured that I was, indeed, old. Well. I didn't even turn *fifty* until the end of that decade, so I really got ahead of myself. What's left after you've worn purple pantsuits and red hats? Lots, as it turns out.

<u>*Yesterday's News...Sunny Side Up*</u>

Do you suppose, when you read these columns of mine, that I'm one of those twinkly, dimpled little old ladies who always has a kind word for everyone? Or do you see through the veneer to the real me?

While I <u>am</u> a little old lady, it's not apple pie or sugarplums that get me to the keyboard. No, the motivation for my writing often comes from something in the newspaper (hence, the title of the column) that just makes me so mad that I could spit nails. I'll storm in here to my desk with venom spewing. Pounding out my vituperative rant and pointing out the idiocy of whatever poor fool has caught my eye, I'll denigrate his parentage, *literacy and common sense. I'll take his pathetic little proposal and tear it to shreds while advising him on where it might best be stored. Oh, I have fun!*

But then, reality sets in. Even though I've yet to meet the editor of our paper, I have a pretty good idea that he'd frown on R-rated content, so I start the clean up.

My intent is to try to voice frustrations that are felt by so many of us who sometimes think "for the luvvapete!! Am I the only one who sees the madness of this?!" No, you're not. And if you're of a mind to, you could spend all day every day in online chat rooms carrying on in a manner that would get your mouth washed out with soap if your mother could hear you.

We all have frustrations with the way of the world, probably from the caveman forward that's been true. I think it's healthy when we can get together in the corner cafe over a cup of coffee and solve the world's problems before we get on with our day. I don't think that there's one thing healthy about the tone of the discourse that people allow themselves online.

There are a few people whom I know to be pleasant, affable company in person but are vulgar, vicious chowderheads online. Some at least use aliases to disguise their bile, but more and more often you see people just

3

feeling free to come completely unhinged using their own names. Trust me when I tell you that writing under a byline will keep most of us on the straight and narrow.

Until my rants are cleaned up, no one sees (or would want to see) them except me. I want to have something go out there that a person can read and say to themselves "Yeah, I've had that thought, too; at least someone else feels the same way." There's a certain comfort in knowing that you're not the only one who sees a situation as being skewed. My style is to do it a bit more gently so that you who lean the same way aren't made to feel like Neanderthals for agreeing with me. Of course, those of you who don't agree with me ARE Neanderthals...Oh! Wait, this is the final draft! Be nice.

———————

Fifty is not old. If you're in good health, 50 and 60 are *great* decades (and they go faster than you can imagine, so make the most of them!). But if you are never able to snap yourself out of a slump like I experienced at 49 or are afflicted with some debilitating illness, old age can seem like an eternity. Certainly a good attitude can help, but it can also be hard to maintain in the face of suffering.

Seventy is beginning to look like the real thing. Old. The world and everything in it are changing at a lightning pace, health can begin to be a much more fragile thing than you'd ever imagined and people you love are falling like flies. At eighty, all of this change and disintegration speeds up and at ninety, you have to carefully pick and choose which things you can attempt to monitor much less participate in.

I so admire people my age and into their 90's who present the world with a visage that says that you can still be *you* at any age and find joy in life. Those people have the ability to gloss over the ravages that time inflicts on them and to make the determination that they're going to *make the best of* and *be happy in* every day. They're also givers; people who pay it forward by helping others in ways large and small. Volunteering our endless time is a great way to give back, meet people who believe in at least some of the things we do and to help keep our brains from turning to mush.

And my brain's gotten pretty mushy. I'd rather have a choice between yard work and 'real' work, but even though I'd like to be productive again, I realize that my decision-making skills just can't be trusted like they once could. I simply have no patience for any of this and, while I may *be* a jackass, standing here being pummeled by old age seems like a sorry choice.

Leslie Baker

Advice: When your parent's or grandparent's birthdays roll around, make your call to them as early in the day as you think they'll be fully caffeinated. Don't wait until later; your call will be the highlight of their day and they'll want to brag about and enjoy it all day.

...2...PARTNERS

Waking up with a stranger sounds like such a bawdy adventure, doesn't it? But it's not as wickedly exciting if that stranger is the same person you've been waking up with for forty or fifty years.

I've heard tales from women (of course!) feeling that they just don't understand who they're married to anymore. Whether their husbands have actually developed strange new habits or their same old quirks have suddenly begun to grate is unclear. Men don't discuss these things (even with other men, apparently.) The only time a male friend has ever opened up to me about something like this was when his wife was in the throes of Parkinson's and he was at his wit's end and grieving their situation.

If it's Parkinson's, a stroke, Alzheimer's or some other long-term affliction that's causing your significant other to behave in ways foreign to you both and to your relationship, life is going to be really rotten for a while. I'm so sorry to have to say that, but there's just no way to put a rosy spin on those hideous diseases or their impact on whole families. Get a good Hospice organization involved as soon as humanly possible and force yourself to keep up some outside interests are the most helpful things I can suggest; it's not enough, I know.

If women of a certain age are feeling that they're waking up to a stranger (without the perks) it's possible (though we'll never know for sure) that men are feeling it, too. Maybe we who survived a mid-life crisis in our forties or fifties are now going through a late-life crisis. Maybe every 25 years or so, we go through a bit of a shift in our needs, wants, personalities, expectations, etc. That was enough of a rut (or chasm) in the road the *first* time we hit it that many marriages didn't survive. Now, we're old, grouchy and impatient. We're also tired and most of us look at the idea of ending a marriage and starting over in our dotage as a ludicrous possibility.

Hey, this is completely off topic, but humor me. One of the things I most dislike about the fact that each and every one of us have our own cell phone in our pocket at all times is that you never have the phone answered by the 'wrong' person anymore. Remember when you'd call your friend and his wife would pick up the phone? There was usually a nice little chat with her before the phone was handed over. I miss that feeling that there's a 'couples' connection among the four (or three) of you.

Yesterday's News...Good Enough

The addiction that hounded me for years is under control. I guess that you're never truly cured, but I can finally go for several days before I have to Just Say No.

Yes, I'm a recovering Perfectionist. Where does something like this come from? While I was raised in a family who all kept things neat and tidy, no one was as loony as I became about water spots on chrome or laser-straight picture frames.

I've always loved moving and have a friend who, for years, has amused himself by coming into my 'new' house and seeing if he can find the phone book or scissors in the kitchen. This little game entertains him because he's always said that 'Leslie is so organized; things are where it makes the most sense.' Because Terry is a pretty logical guy himself (except for his hare-brained politics!) he has about a 99% first-guess solve rate.

It's long been said that perfection is the enemy of the good enough and that only boring women have perfect houses. Well, for years, I just unconsciously strove for perfection. Understand that these OCD standards I imposed only on myself with zero expectation of them in anyone else. I could be completely happy and wallow in someone else's whirlwind housekeeping, gardening or thought processes. Just not mine.

The 'C' word probably figured into my mania for perfection. After all, if there was nothing else that I could Control, I could at least make sure that my vitamin bottles were perfectly aligned, right?

The incident that finally snapped me out of perfection for perfection's sake came ten or fifteen years ago. I was fixing a house prior to flipping it and the huge wall-mounted mirror for one of the bathrooms arrived on site just in the nick of time. As the guys prepared to hoist it into place, I noticed that a tiny piece of the silvering was missing. Aaarrgh. Special order glass, house on the market tomorrow, no time for this! I went out to the car, opened a piece of chewing gum and taped its shiny, silver wrapper over that damned hole.

This was so not me. The guys who'd watched me take a fit over trifles like this were bug-eyed. Maybe their astonishment was the trigger that helped me over the hump. I began to see that 'good-enough' is sometimes all you need, that perfectionism isn't all it's cracked up to be. Boy, what a feeling of freedom!

Now, I won't lie and tell you that I've reached my goal of becoming an unrepentant slob. If the house-fire hasn't

10

reached the second floor, you're still going to find my bed made and I confess to having little jars of touch-up paint always at the ready, but you absolutely wouldn't want to eat off my floors anymore. I'm relaxing into this good-enough philosophy!

———————

A second or third marriage in your fifties, sixties or seventies is exciting and doable if you're both in good health and neither of you is looking for a meal ticket. If you're a widower at almost any age, another marriage can be a gift under the right circumstances.

But divorce at 75? Just because he won't put his TV tray away? Or you're sick to death of having *her* undies drying on *your* towel? That's a heavy lift.

Many things contribute to that feeling of 'who the hell *is* this person?!' Maybe one of the most pervasive is failing hearing; as simplistic as that sounds. When things have to be repeated all the time, when one of you is in denial about losing your hearing and tries to fake it, resulting in often wildly garbled conversations, tensions can mount. *Nobody* wants the bother, expense or appearance of hearing aids, but when your interactions with others have become so difficult that you begin to avoid conversation, feel defensive when you're misunderstood and see that your relationships are faltering, it's time to look into the options. A new partner isn't going to solve the problem.

Changing household and relationship responsibilities can also cause tension. One of the first times this nails most couples is when one or both of you retire. Having your sweetie underfoot 24/7 is a lot different than having him show up at 6PM and toddle off again at 7AM. Routines are radically changed for both of you and it's almost impossible to not get tight-lipped about being told the right way to run that vacuum cleaner or that the sound of the #%@# television all day long is not going over well. If you're able to afford a month-long trip together right after the retirement party, it might help you acclimate to the constant togetherness before you have to incorporate it into your home. It's a hard transition, though, so try to talk about it openly and nicely before it becomes explosive. We all need our space.

The effects of various new disabilities are another stressor. If she's always done the grocery shopping but can no longer drive, he's going to screw it up. Guaranteed. If she goes along to the store, they're likely to argue over the way he loads the cart or the route he chooses to take through the store. If he's always been the one to call the kids on Sundays but can't distinguish voices on the phone anymore, she has to change her role in that scenario. Sure, they're little things, but when you're old, patience is at a premium when things keep piling on. And it's hard to cede 'your' jobs to each other; you feel like a useless old failure.

Your kids are certainly a consideration in changing relationships at any age. And they usually don't want to know any more than the bare minimum about the mechanics of their parents' (with or without step-parents involved) marriage. Until one of you sets your robe afire, they'd like to ignore the whole parents-getting-older thing.

I wish I had an 'Abracadabra' fix for this, but I don't. Deep breathing, time-outs and some weed might be the answer. If you decide to try medical or recreational marijuana for the first time or because you remember how mellowing a little toke was 50 years ago, let me offer a word of caution.

Some people I know were laughing with their younger friend about something as he painted their kitchen. Dope came into the conversation and they said they'd enjoyed it but hadn't had any for many years. When he left for the evening, the young fellow generously left them a joint and said he'd be back tomorrow to finish painting. My friends were so excited! Well. That stuff put them on their asses. They were actually frightened by the strength of their reactions and said there was *nothing* mellow about the experience. What a bummer!

So if you decide to try today's dope, be aware that it's a whole different weed than it was when we were young. *And*, (I hate to keep reminding you of this) we're *old*; many of us are on any number of medications that can interact with the dope. So ask your doctor, be sure that you get the mildest form available and approach it gingerly until you get a feel for how it's going to affect you. That's what *I'm* gonna do!

Advice: Skip this if you're a city dweller. If coyotes, gophers, etc. around your barn or storeroom are bedeviling you, make a perimeter trail around the structure with well-used (scooped) cat litter. It's a great deterrent but you don't want it near your house or outdoor living areas.

...3...TECHNOLOGY

Most people, young and old, are equally impacted by the technology in our lives, but the young line up around the block to get their hands on it. For those of us born to phones with cords and typewriters without them, the transitions are usually less welcome. Many of us will hang on to our old flip-phone to the bitter end and *never* learn to use most of the features on our shiny new damnable Smartphone.

I love a lot of the tech in my life, but it's a rare day when some aspect of it doesn't just piss me off to the nth degree. I would never bother to write if not for Steve Jobs; the ease of editing on a computer makes even the laziest of us able to play with words to our heart's content. What I don't love are the endless 'updates' that you'd expect to *improve* your devices, but which rarely do much except screw up something that had been working just fine.

The fact that we oldsters have been as flexible as we have in adapting to new technologies was brought home when

I realized that I was fifty years old when Google was born. Lordy.

Yesterday's News...Tech and the Handyman

I recently had a couple of tense moments with our longtime friend/handyman who was here replacing the toilet seats in our house. He was mumbling under his breath (very politely, he doesn't swear like a fishmonger the way I do) and struggling with what would ordinarily be a quickie job. When I asked if he'd read the instructions I'd fished out of the trash, he looked at me like I'd spoken Swahili; he's installed countless of these things in his long life.

These were not high-tech self-closing, light-emitting, music-streaming, bidet-toilet seats, they were as garden variety as it's possible to find. And yet, some rocket scientist had seen fit to design a different attachment method. Not improved, just different. Why on earth?!

Well. I think I've found the answer to not only the toilet seat question but to my almost daily queries of "why the Sam Hill did they change that?!"

Whether it's the soap dispenser in the dishwasher, the front-loading clothes washer that can't be closed when not in use lest it mildew, or the way hotel room keys operate, things that worked reliably for years on end are suddenly redesigned every time the calendar changes.

For some time, I've blamed all of this mania to change things just for the sake of change, regardless of whether or not it actually <u>improves</u> anything, on young techies who have to justify sitting at their design stations (or on the couch in their jammies with a latte and their laptop) for eight hours a day. Now, as I look at it calmly, I believe that I'm right.

The government has long been a reliable provider of jobs with indecipherable titles in mysterious departments that do little but provide a nice retirement income to the occupants of those positions and there's no reason to expect <u>that</u> to change. But in most other walks of life, the computerization of manufacturing, communications and fast-food positions; new minimum wage requirements which have employers cutting staff along with the advent of Amazon and it's like, means that there are fewer and fewer jobs every day.

Voila! What we see is the reemergence of "The Tinkerer." Before Man Caves, men retired to their tool benches in the garage to fiddle around and avoid helping with the dishes.

Then Bill Gates and Steve Jobs connected garages and <u>technology</u> in our mindset.

Now, tinkering with technology and actual products for no reason other than to kill time making changes to others' inventions is a profession. My Daddy would be tickled to know that tinkering has been elevated to the status of 'Career.'

Envision a tall, triangle-shaped bottle of shampoo with the cap at the wide bottom. Now, feel that full, heavy, wet flash of brilliance in your hand while you're in the shower; try to get some of the shampoo into your hand, then close the lid so you can set it down. To the floor, Alice, to the floor.

I suspect that new designs are never field tested anymore. That shampoo, the dishwasher soap dispenser, a certain photo editing program would never make it to market if anyone had actually tried to <u>use</u> a prototype in a real life setting. Instead, these ideas seem to go directly from the CAD program on the techie's laptop to market.

The rest of us are the recipients. Maybe learning to swear in Swahili will relieve some of the tension?

———

Tech is an area that separates us from our friends who are only a tiny bit older or younger. A little younger and they may text but they can't text photos. A little older and they probably don't do either. Many who are older don't email on a computer much less on their phone. This causes me fits when I have to remember who does what when I want to relay a message!

I was so impressed recently when a friend was using Alexa to control her music selections at home and thought 'I'm going to go right home and work on learning to do that myself,' but the cat needed brushing, so I forgot all about Alexa and Siri. Oh, but I did run across a great website for oldsters trying to grapple with Twitter or smartphones: TechBoomers is aimed at us! It really helps.

The older you are, the less likely you are to bother learning to do more than the most rudimentary things with phone *or* desktop. Learning *anything* new (or *retaining* it) as you get older is harder than it used to be and when it's technology that's going to change again in a month, many of us have developed a 'hell with it' attitude. We'll get along with the basics but many of the shiny new objects are just not that enticing anymore.

This sorry attitude can contribute to our growing isolation, but many of us are bored blind by technology and just want the simplest damned things to work simply. Sadly, I think that those days are behind us.

Advice: Stairs Suck. As our bodies get older or sloppy from pregnancy, our bellies can get ugly. If you often have reason to climb stairs, suck in your gut for the whole climb up or down. Remember that Stairs Suck and do it, it can really help.

...4...RELIGION

Wouldn't you think that we'd all be settled in our belief systems by the time we're old? I'm pretty annoyed with religion right now. Not with God, but at some of the asinine ways people handle their belief in Him.

I was raised Episcopalian, raised my son nominally Catholic (for which he still carries a bit of a grudge) and went through my 20's, 30's and 40's kind of ignoring the whole topic.

When my son was in his late teens, I received a midnight phone call telling me to meet the ambulance at the hospital's emergency entrance. Matt and a friend had been in a single car accident out in the sticks and were both going to be transported to the hospital.

I got to the crash site before the ambulance left and followed it to town.

(Matt told me later that the ambulance driver had said to him on the trip to town 'Your Mom's a really good driver.' That and two similar comments from fighter pilots my dad's age have buoyed me in my love of driving for my whole life!)

The kids were both OK enough to be treated and released (and...hallelujah...were clean and sober) so, once my heart rate returned to normal, it seemed like a totaled car was the worst of it. The next day, Phillip (who later became my husband) and I went to the wrecking yard to empty the car before it went under the ball. Well. Seeing that mangled, bloody clutch of metal and rubber in broad daylight sent me right over the edge. After the hysteria subsided, I thanked God in ways that were wholly inadequate to the blessing he'd bestowed on all of us. I promised Him that I'd begin wearing a cross as soon as I could track down a lovely one and I did. Pathetic offering, but it was what I could do. I don't think that, some years later, as I got fat and the cross began irritating my wrinkled old cleavage, God gave a damn that I put it away.

Did any of you see a recent "Non Sequitur" cartoon? (I love that thing!) This one showed God, lightning bolt drooping at his side, viewing the apocalypse below saying, "OK, lesson learned...Next time, no religion."

I think that organized religion can be detrimental when it gets so insular that there's a 'right' and a 'wrong' way to believe in God. As long as our different faiths don't compel us to *destroy* each other, we should be able to co-exist peaceably.

Yesterday's News...Muslims

I don't know any Muslims. Not by design, just a matter of circumstance. Having lived all but about 5 intermittent years of my life in little, rural towns, there simply haven't been many opportunities to meet them.

When 9/11/2001 hit, I lived in an isolated mountain town in California. Like everyone, Phillip and I were horrified and numbed by that unprecedented event. After checking in with my then 21 year-old son and going to a community church service to be with neighbors and share our shock and grief, one of the first things I remember that we discussed was that Muslims and anyone else who wore headgear that didn't involve a brim or a bill were going to be targets of hate.

That proved to be sadly prophetic. All over the country, there were and continue to be ugly, ignorant incidents that are entirely unacceptable.

In the years since 9/11, I've read a number of books toward trying to educate myself about the basics of Islam and trying to learn how to differentiate between garden variety Muslims and Islamic Extremists. I'm a long way from getting there. If anything, I feel more confused than when I began this odyssey.

How are we to understand this faith-based terror that is shrouding the world? I have to believe that if, in this era, Christian Extremists began slaughtering those who didn't agree with their idea of 'God,' I'd have to re-examine my identity as a Christian.

At the very least, I'd have to join with other Christians to initiate a plan to differentiate us from the lunatics doing the mayhem and try to make it clear to the world that the radicals did NOT speak for the rest of us. If that proved to be either not the case or an undoable task, I'd have to find a new way to define my faith in God.

This is what I don't understand: why isn't there more visible outrage from mainstream American Muslims? Why don't we read more of their defense of their religion? Why don't we see an explanation, from within the Muslim community, of the difference between them and the extremists? There may be explanations in scholarly publications that I don't see, but we everyday people <u>need</u> to see those explanations. (For anyone along this same journey, I'd recommend books by Ayaan Hirsi Ali who the Wall Street Journal calls "...the most *dangerous foe of Islamist extremism in the Western world").*

We NEED to understand why we shouldn't fear that the Muslims down the street would, if push comes to shove, side with the extremists rather than with their Christian neighbors in defending our way of life. Would they take up arms against Islamists in the same way that I would? Or would they shrug and say, "Oh, well, maybe the Quran <u>DID</u> say to kill the infidels"? I'm pretty uncomfortable at not having any idea how this might shake out.

I'm just as uncomfortable, though, with judging other Americans on their choice of religion.

––––––––––

Faith in God, if we're going to partake, should be a <u>comfort</u> in our old age. But I've seen just the opposite effect in several of my nearest and dearest. My two oldest friends (*they're* not old of course, but our *friendship* is) have become active in two different churches that have them whipped into very different frenzies. These gals are heavily invested in the coming of Armageddon (though their texts each have different terminologies for it) and the unspeakable suffering that everybody but they and fellow members of <u>*that*</u> denomination are going to endure. According to them, *their* religion (and, remember that these are radically different churches that these two belong to, so they certainly don't agree with *each other*) is the only one that's got it right and will spare them the hellfire to come. Well, Christ Almighty. Is *this* bringing comfort and peace to anyone?!

Another long-time friend was born into an Italian Catholic family but, terrified by the gruesome images of Christ on the Cross, staged a very youthful rebellion against Catholicism. She's explored Buddhism and many other (you name it!) unconventional ways to re-establish a connection to God and spirituality, but, nearing 80, is still searching and somewhat unsettled.

In her final years, my Mom, who'd been a very involved and generous Methodist all her life, lost connection with her church. (My Mom was actually my stepmother and not involved raising me...lucky gal!) She still liked to attend the Christmas Cantata, but several successive pastors neglected visits to her even as she became more and more homebound before dying at 95. Her feelings were terribly hurt (as would be those of the pastors had they known that her very magnanimous donation to the church was summarily scratched from her will). Those men, and one woman to whom my stepbrother referred as 'The Cheerleader,' really soured her on the whole bunch and she wanted no clergy involved even with her burial.

My Mom missed church and she took to watching Joel Osteen on Sunday mornings. At first, while with her on a weekend, I'd sort of roll my eyes and watch with her just to be polite. I found that I enjoyed him enough that I began watching him at home, too. My husband (after first rolling *his* eyes) started staying in the room until it's become a Sunday morning habit for us. I feel an intimacy with God that I'd been missing in my life; just having a weekly occasion that prods me to remember God has been a gift; I find myself making more time for and feeling more natural with prayer than ever before in my life. Early in life, I'd gotten it into my head that prayers of thanks were always in order, but to ask for help from God was, somehow, a sign of weakness or ingratitude. Joel has helped me to look at that differently and to actually ask for some help or mercy now and then.

Phillip and I make a point of immediately discussing the main points that we took from Joel's message that day. If we don't do so, we don't remember it any more than we remember to buy eggs. In a recent message, Osteen exhorted us to not let life steal our joy and that was so simple and true that I thought "this is why we listen to this guy for 30 minutes a week."

Yes, certainly we are aware of the fact that Joel is a very rich man who wants others to support his mega-church with their offerings when he passes the plate. We don't contribute (nor did my Mom), but we benefit, so who's cheating who, here?

The single recurring gripe I've had with Joel's message is that he doesn't deal with the topic of death. I understand that his goal is to be uplifting and positive in that half-hour but when I have a friend dying and I hear a minister saying that healing is on the horizon (when it sure as hell *isn't* in her case), the only way I've been able to make that work is to look at death as the final form of healing. When a preacher reassures us that 'promotion and favor' are on the way and we know that another friend's stage 4 lung cancer isn't likely to magically vanish, the only way for me to take comfort from faith in God is to see promotion to Heaven as the ultimate in favor.

Most of us struggle to read our spouse's handwriting. By what logic do we suppose that the Bible was, over as many as 3,500 years, correctly deciphered from oral tradition, many dialects of many languages, on stone or papyrus to become what's on our shelves today? Literacy was in even shorter supply then than now and those few scribes were dealing with pretty complex topics. I'd guess that most of the 30 or so people credited with interpreting the Old Testament/Torah and maybe 10 people contributing to the New Testament meant well and didn't intentionally make attributions to God or misquote Jesus in ways that they knew to be bogus. But there are just too many arguments to be had in trying to agree on what a contemporary version of the Bible 'really' says for me to suppose that it's come down to us unadulterated. Even modern movements with the goal of restoration to the 'original' Christianity have splintered because they can't agree on definitions and interpretations of their *own* re-interpretive texts.

A well-intentioned Bible study group can damned near come to blows in arguing their views of what the Bible says and means. So much of this discussion feels fragile and fear-based (to say nothing of strident!) Could it have been different with those early writer/interpreters? Who won *those* arguments? Why? How much compromise was involved? I fully believe in God; the Bible, not so much.

A dear friend of mine died a few years ago and I still miss her. Alice had been raised Jewish but at some stage, opted out of religion altogether. As close as we were, I never heard the reason for her having left the faith of her birth and I've wished many times that I could talk with her about it now. Did she essentially come to the same comfort level as I have: believing in God but being skeptical of 'religion'? One of my favorite glimpses of Heaven is sitting with Alice and marveling over all of the things we *didn't* know about God, faith (and a whole lot of other stuff!) while we were on Earth. I'd love to hear her take on the CS Lewis thought: 'You don't have a soul. You are a Soul. You have a body.'

Funeral services have begun to give way to 'Celebrations of Life' and I see that as a positive commentary on the ways in which our society is trying to embrace death into the full circle that we've always known life makes. If we can genuinely and openly celebrate our loved one's well lived life and ascension to Heaven, it doesn't immediately lessen our own loss and grief, but it can help us to heal.

Services for our dead *are* important; it's gotten fairly routine to hear that the deceased has requested no services. That's so *selfish!* Whoever died may have had reasons for not wanting a service, may even have felt that it's the humble thing to request no gathering in their honor. But, unless you live far away from all of your family and friends when you die, I strongly disagree.

Those of us who are left behind are the ones who need that time of coming together; it's for *us* more than for the guy in the casket or urn. Often there will be a disparate group attending a service whose only connection to each other was through the fellow who died. Some of these people may never see each other again, but for that day, the mingling of the love and regard they share for the departed is healing to them and necessary to their journey forward. And if you're such a gnarly old toot that everybody's *glad* you're gone, then we can hold a helluva party and say nanner-nanner to your wishes!

Grieving and healing is a long process; there are many factors that can magnify or minimize the loss in particular circumstances, but if there's a way to avoid the whole damned thing, I haven't heard of it.

My friend Mary recently lost her twin brother. I would be torn asunder to lose my beloved brother and have no concept of how that feeling would be compounded in losing a twin; it's been hard for me to express the fullness of my sorrow for Mary because I cannot feel the uniqueness of her loss. The same is true of the loss of a baby or child of any age; the grief of a parent is something that those of us blessed enough to have not experienced it are at a loss to fully comprehend.

My husband lost his eighteen-year-old son fifty years ago during The Pueblo Incident. My grandmother lost her eighteen-year-old son during WWII. Both Phillip and Gramma healed and lived full lives, but the loss was never far from the surface for either of them. Millions of people have to cope with what has to be life's worst loss, that of a grown and beloved child. To do so without some reliance on God sounds impossible to me.

How do those with no belief in God or heaven approach impending death? The old saw about there being no atheists in foxholes comes to mind. To feel cut-and-dried in your opinion that the deed's done and the dirt's next must appeal to a lot of people, but I would find it terribly lonely and hollow; I'm happy to have God to cling to.

My four old buddies, my Mom and I are examples of the divergent paths that we can take toward religion late in life. Whether it's the church around the corner or a TV preacher, I hope that most people have found a way to connect with and be grateful to God on some kind of regular basis.

Advice: One of the smartest people I've ever known made me feel like a rocket scientist when she didn't realize that the recessed sharp point on the cap of a tube of ointment or gel is to pierce the damnable foil that seals the tube.

...5...MONEY

I've mentioned being grateful for an abundant life. There are an awful lot of oldsters who barely survive financially. I know of one couple who live a very modest life (though upscale from living in a box on a sidewalk) yet are, in their 90's, still sweetly in love and happy. They're a religious pair and I've wondered if their faith helps them to look at life with such grace?

Other folks made a couple of poor financial choices or were badly impacted by the last (*most recent*, you know there's another one right around the corner) recession at crucial, late in the earning years times that abruptly snatched them from what had been envisioned as a comfortable retirement and plunged them into scraping by. Making risky investments that promise to double your money is awfully tempting when you're afraid that you don't have enough socked away at the end of your working years. Thank God for Wal-Mart who keeps a lot of fragile, destitute old souls employed when no one else will bother with them.

Some, of course, began with terrible choices almost from the get-go and have always lived life teetering on the brink. In a way, they're the ones who survive penury best because they've long known how to game the system and find a meal or the rent when the rest of us wouldn't have a clue where to look.

Whether from bad luck or bad choices, being poor in your dotage must be almost unendurable. There's nothing easy about old age anyway and the stress of poverty besides is a terrible fate.

Having a target on your back is just part of being old. Most of us, no matter our best intentions, are woefully behind the curve when it comes to technology. The ones way ahead of that curve are the ones who see oldsters as easy pickin's for the scam of the week. Whether you don't watch (or pay attention to) the evening news or whether you just forget all about it when the oven timer dings, you are ready to be had. And you're *not* going to enjoy it.

We've found that the very best way to avoid telemarketers (and politicians, yay!) is to *not answer the phone if the caller isn't in your 'contacts' list.* If your cell phone doesn't show a name you recognize, let it go to voicemail. If it's a legitimate call, you'll find a message and if it's not, you may have dodged a bullet.

Being scammed doesn't have to originate with your tech tools. There's a class of people who make their living by targeting the vulnerable and gullible of a certain age. None of us like to think that we aren't still as sharp as when we were making business decisions day in and day out, but whether from isolation, medication or just confusion and exhaustion from the pace of the world, we're not.

'Kids' in their 40's and 50's are shocked the first time they hear that Dad paid $1,500. to a nice young man who offered to pave his driveway with 'leftover' blacktop only to take the money and run leaving behind a gooey mess in a driveway that's in worse shape than before. When something like this happens more than once (when a stove burner is left on or the door is left unlocked) is when a lot of us end up in the kids' back bedroom or in a 'home.' Being able to discern a scam from a business deal is harder than ever and especially for those a few years removed from the business world.

Yesterday's News...Birthdays and Death Days

This year marked my first Mother's Day without my Mom.

Are there any of us old enough to not feel orphaned when we lose our last parent? I have a husband, a son and daughter-in-law, a brother and more wonderful friends than I probably deserve. But my Mom, Dot, is gone and there's a hole in my heart.

Dot's birthday always fell within a few days of Mother's Day. Last year was her 95th and there was a big whing-ding which she fully enjoyed. It was a month before her unexpected death and the last time I saw her.

Now, I'm tasked with following some of my own advice. In the years when I was a Hospice volunteer, I always encouraged my surviving clients who had lost a loved one to allow themselves to acknowledge the first anniversary date of the death. After that 1st year, though, my experience has taught me that it's the <u>birthday</u> of a lost loved one that is a joyous time at which to remember them and to give thanks for all they brought to our lives.

The anniversary of a death is bereft of positive associations. I believe that my Mom, for instance, would want us to celebrate her birthday every year and to just ignore that dreadful date that marks her death. At the first year, the death date can't be ignored; it slugs you in the gut. But it's surprisingly easy to put that date aside in future years; to give yourself permission to do what your loved one would probably want you to do and to honor them on a joyful date.

Dot was, technically, my stepmother. In every other respect, she was the Mom I loved. I rarely lived with my troubled birth mother and was primarily raised by my spectacular Gramma. When Daddy married Dot it was like the missing piece in our family puzzle had been found. My brother and I were young adults by then, but Dot opened her arms to us and always treated us as if we were her own sons' siblings. It's a real gift to have that kind of heart. Dot, at her death, had been my Mom for more years than Mother had been at the time of her death, yet so many people seem to have the feeling that she was 'only' my step-mother and just don't get that I lost my Mom.

I hope that I'll learn from this to be more understanding and sympathetic to the 'step' side of parenting in other people's lives.

It's hard to find the upside of grief. I'm happy to report, however, that, a year later, I can see my Mom's dimples again, and hear her adorable, little-girl laugh. This is how I'll remember her, feeling the loss always, but my memories treasured and held with gratitude.

Recently, a small investment property that I'd wanted to get my hands on for several years came on the market. I wrote an offer that was sure to be accepted but then backed out before submitting it. Why? Because the same lack of qualified help for the project that had made me quit working ten years ago is still the norm. I want to work again so badly that I almost lost my ass by living in la-la-land instead of facing reality. I snapped to in time, but this incident really rocked me. I'm never going to have the mental or financial wherewithal to work again and it's a life-altering realization. Who *am* I now?

In the last 20 years or so, there have been innumerable articles in newspapers and magazines giving people graphs and calculators to determine how much money they'll need to have socked away in order to live a comfortable retirement. The easiest thing to do is to ignore them because you almost never come away feeling anything but a panicked desperation. Trust Dave Ramsay and your own common sense would be my advice. In my limited acquaintance, I've known several people who've made themselves sick stewing because they, at 70, didn't have a million dollars in a coffee can. No; but with Social Security, Medicare, no debt, a reasonable lifestyle and a small pension of some sort they were doing fine. Certainly without *some* savings, you can't absorb a crisis, but try not to ruin your last years with worry that may be unfounded. Swallow the fear, talk to someone who isn't trying to sell you anything and assess the situation rationally.

Please don't be so afraid of what you'll learn that you don't educate yourself on the realities of geriatric finances. You've worked for and paid taxes on that money; try to be your own best advocate in situations involving it.

If you own your home and are feeling stretched financially, you might reconsider a Reverse Mortgage. I was dead-set against them when they first became popular, but I do think they've been improved. They're not for everyone, but if you can use the extra monthly income, do what's best for you. Not your kids, *you*. If you've raised your kids right and they're self-supporting, you have no obligation to leave them anything at the expense of your own comfort and happiness in your final years. They'd probably agree with this.

Hey, did you know that, in at least some Arizona banks, it's forbidden to keep cash in your safe deposit box at the bank? Boy, *that'll* show those drug dealers, won't it? 'Lets just screw with the 92% of honest Americans,' decided someone, 'in order to make life harder for the 8% of shysters in their midst'. Lordy. I was introduced to this fact a few years ago when the manager of my bank branch called me and, in a round-a-bout way asked if I was keeping cash in my safe deposit box. For a couple of years, I'd been taking out a few hundred dollars cash when I had it to spare in my checking account and putting it in the box at the bank. They'd been monitoring my activity and called me on it! That was a creepy and infuriating feeling, let me tell you. I keep thinking that I'm going to get one of those exploding 'snake in a can' paper snakes to put in that box and just never use it again. I'd love to be a fly on the wall when they open it!

And don't get me started on 'structuring' laws! Again, we honest folk get messed with because the Feds can't find a way to catch crooks without making life harder for us! Look into this aspect of banking before you withdraw $12,000 in cash to buy your grandson a car.

I've considered filing an 'age-discrimination' suit against banks in general. I won't do it because I'm A] fervently opposed to most lawsuits; and B] too tired to bother; but I wish *somebody* would. I'm fairly tech-savvy, but a lot of people my age and older aren't and the banks have been cutting back their on-site services until it's almost impossible to get any banking done unless you're willing and able to do it online. This is really dangerous to a lot of seniors who don't have the knowledge to protect themselves, their information and their money in online transactions. Yes, I realize that actual accounts are FDIC insured, but the long, drawn-out turmoil and stress of a hack are just one more insult/injury situation that old people are subjected to.

There's no glib, perky way to dismiss poverty in old age. As I sit here in my cozy office writing this, I *know* that I'm lucky. The worst financial worry we have is that The Socialist Republic of California will bail on my husband's pension fund; well, there's not one damned thing that we can do about that, so neither of us is inclined to wring our hands and fret. Like Armageddon and arthritis, if it happens, we'll deal with it then.

Advice: A method to help you fall asleep: Don't turn out the light and think about tomorrow's schedule or anything else on which your actions can have ANY impact. Review the chapters you've just read in a murder mystery or the film you saw yesterday. Think of NOTHING having to do with you or anyone you know.

...6...BETRAYAL OF THE BODY

A ging is a bitch, no two ways about it. Trust me, I *know* that I'm one of the lucky ones. As I write this, I can still walk, drive, do my own gardening, string full sentences together most of the time, eat what I like (if it's no later than 5PM), and wear ordinary underwear, though it's not the sexy, high-cut stuff of yore.

Many people my age are in much more dire straits. Lots of us have oxygen tanks at the ready, 'incontinent' undergarments, catheters, walkers, dreadful diets, weird growths and discolorations all over our bodies, the strength and stamina of bubbles, barely able to balance on flat ground, hair that grows where it shouldn't and *not* where it should, humiliating digestive issues...I'm sure you have your own list of gripes. Remember the scenes in the old movie "10" where the pastor's deaf old housekeeper kept shuffling through the room farting like a racehorse and the poor dog got yelled at for it to spare her dignity? Well, we get it now, don't we?

Speaking of balance issues...The Bathroom Massacre is a specter that many of us ancients fear. Taking a shower can be a real challenge when you get ridiculously dizzy by just closing your eyes and turning a bit to reach for the shampoo. I've had to school myself to do everything *very* slowly and deliberately so I don't go crashing down in a bloody cascade of shattered glass shower doors. What a pain in the ass. BUT before you and the kids decide to install a walk-in-tub or a stair-lift in order to facilitate your 'aging in place' please do a realistic assessment of the situation. If you're only one more fall or other catastrophe away from a care facility, please consider carefully not only the initial expense (many thousands of dollars for a tub *or* a stair-lift) and household upheaval but, in most cases, the removal expense at the eventual listing for sale of the house; these items are rarely considered a marketable feature.

No wonder so many of us are cranky and impatient; the simplest things have turned into marathons of preparedness. Every now and then when we're sitting in one of our favorite breakfast cafes, Phillip and I see one of two other couples who are also regulars. We watch them (occasionally offering to get a door or something that's not too intrusive) struggle just to get out of their vehicles, get their walkers or canes in place and begin the trek. The one spouse who is in marginally better condition is trying to help the other without being in his/her way as they hobble in and have breakfast. Then the whole process is reversed to get back into the car, get home and go through the entire undertaking again just to get into the house. It's exhausting to watch, it must be totally draining to live it. And yet, these brave souls keep making the effort to live their lives in some semblance of normalcy. I'm in awe of them, I cannot imagine having that kind of courage and determination.

That sort of drama is probably one factor in so many of us becoming hermits in our old age; you just begin to feel that there's not one damned thing that's worth the effort.

Yesterday's News...Cancer Scams

For years, I've refused to donate to anything having to do with cancer. Why? Because there's just way too much money being made to justify a full-spectrum cure for cancer.

A recent article has perfectly mirrored my rationale.

The excellent piece in a national paper noted that "Drug companies promise a chance to live longer to boost sales. Hospitals woo paying customers with ads that appeal to patients' fears and hopes."

We've all seen the ads on TV for huge, gleaming beacon-of-hope facilities whose sole reason for being is to treat *cancer. Oh...and to rake in the big bucks. The graph in the article showed that the spending by cancer centers on advertising has increased by 220% since 2005; from 54 million dollars to $173M. That's their ADVERTISING budget!!*

<u>And</u> that's just the cancer care centers. Factor in the massive profits being hauled in by the pharmaceutical industry, by the rampant 'testing/screening' field, by the 'charities' that leech off of the cancer business, and on and on.

As I write this, nobody's much closer to eradicating cancer or even curing any but some of the earliest-stage and a few childhood cancers. (That's after the U.S. has spent over ONE HUNDRED BILLION on <u>research</u> alone since Nixon declared a war on cancer in 1971). Why on earth <u>would</u> they be? What would become of the enormous industries built up around cancer research and care if a cure were announced tomorrow?

Yes, I've had a few friends and relatives who survived for many years after cancer treatment; it does happen, just not nearly often enough. Every day's obituaries tell of more who died way too young.

An even more recent article in the Phoenix paper, written by the CEO of one of the mega-facilities there, quoted him bemoaning the possible cuts in research funding by the National Institutes for Health (that's us, you know). He states that NIH funding is a key economic driver in the health care industry. Well, yeah, THAT'S a key reason to quit throwing my tax dollars so indiscriminately at the industry! Throughout the article are scattered references to cancer rates that continue to rise and a couple of examples of whiz-bang new screening tests that 'look' promising. Another of this fellow's stated concerns is that NIH funding is a 'catalyst for philanthropy.' Help me out, here...they won't be able to attract charitable giving if the pot isn't seeded with our tax dollars? This guy concludes by hoping for a brighter future. Don't we all? But for all the years and money that've been thrown at it, the problem just keeps growing.

A couple of years ago, a valued friend was running in one of these feel-good cancer runs and asked if I'd like to sponsor her. Because she was running in support of a friend of hers who was dealing with cancer, and because I rarely have the opportunity to do one thing for this friend, I made an exception and made a small donation. THERE'S the problem with these bloody damned fund-raisers; it's really hard to say "no" when you've got someone who's barely able to stand, much less run, and they're out there giving it their all because it helps them feel that they're 'fighting back' in the face of a miserable situation. What a sly racket cancer charities are.

We all have the urge to help. I wish I knew of more effective ways to do so; ways that didn't segue into having operating costs that dwarf what actually gets to the people who need it.

Cancer is the biggest, most profitable affliction, but there are certainly other scams out there that are built on our most primal fears and vulnerabilities. Heeding that sage old advice to follow the money will get us to the shysters, but it doesn't seem to be curing the disease.

———

Once a person is diagnosed with a terminal condition, nothing may yet show and they get only a vague expiration date assigned. Having this hanging over one's head often causes them to not share the news with many people because they don't want to be monitored for changes. This situation can also contribute to changes in personality that they struggle to get a handle on. The steady drip-drip of there being ever more areas of life that are affected by such a condition can make a person grouchy as hell and even knowing that all of it makes one unpleasant company doesn't help much to control it.

Remember when our kids were young and Nancy Reagan started the 'Just Say No' program that was quickly accepted by families and communities as a help in deterring drug usage? (Poor Nancy died knowing what a scourge drugs have become in spite of her good intentions) I'd like to see some First Lady revive that program but gear it toward seniors and *their* excessive drug use. I'm grateful that we have some helpful drugs available, but the over-prescription of them is loony. I'm not as concerned about oldsters getting addicted (sheesh, what the hell do you have to lose at *this* stage?) as I am about the interactions with other drugs that can cause symptoms that are worse than the diseases they're supposed to be treating. It's not unusual for a person to have 15 prescriptions on their kitchen counter and I have very little confidence that physicians or pharmacists monitor the interactions before adding a new one. Handing someone 5 sheets of paper telling of the possible side effects pretty much absolves the professionals of any responsibility.

I mentioned earlier that I'd been crazy, but healthy. Well, having lived with what used to be called 'Stage IV Major Depressive Disorder' for about 15 years was just a nightmare. The medications were worse than the condition and the worst of it was that nothing showed. If I tried, in all of my youthful, healthful glory, to define my malady for someone, it was promptly forgotten because I *looked* so well. Some days, I'd rather have been bleeding like a stuck hog so that people could have *seen* that I wasn't just being a wimp (or a lunatic bitch, depending on the day). So, as with the maladies of age, you quit trying to explain it and trundle on.

Have you ever noticed how quick people are to condemn suicide? Certainly, intervention is called for when a young healthy person has hit what feels like the end of the road, but this isn't the part of the book about young, healthy people. Even if it's someone who is otherwise facing a long and agonizing death, many people are absolutely convinced that to bail while you're still able to is 'against God's wishes.' Horse pucky.

There was a story some years ago about a mountain climber out on his own in God's Left Armpit who took a tumble and ended with his arm hopelessly stuck in a rock vise. He had to calculate how long he could wait for help before losing so much strength that he wouldn't be able to cut off his arm with a pocketknife without passing out and bleeding to death. He was totally on his own to make that brutal call on his chance of survival.

In considering suicide, you can feel that you're in an unsurvivable situation; you may feel that you've already cut off all the limbs you can spare. It is not always a selfish decision as is so quickly supposed by those who haven't been there. A person can be in so much psychic or physical pain that the impact of their actions on others doesn't enter their mind.

Did you hear that? The person often doesn't consider and then discard thoughts of their loved ones. <u>*Those thoughts do not enter their minds*</u>. They do not feel or see that there could be other options. Of course, there *are* the people who think '*This'll* show those sonsabitches!' but I suspect they're not quite as serious about the task as the truly desperate.

If the critical state has gone on long enough, the suicidal person *has* had searing conversations with themselves about the effect of their decision on their loved ones. But when the apex is reached, they are the only one in the picture. Bringing the situation to a conclusion is the only focus.

If you're the one left behind in the suicide of a loved one, you will feel like a kicked-to the-curb remnant; that you didn't matter in his life. As hard as it is, try to accept that *you* weren't his focus when he was in the most pain. You will go through the stages of grief caused by all death (acceptance, anger, bargaining, denial and depression) and be miserable. Please get whatever support is available to you and recognize that those grief stages don't come in any set order. You may feel all of them in an hour's time or dwell on one or the other for days at a time for months; it's ugly but normal. The only emotion that you really should put up a fight against is guilt. You didn't do this and, in most cases, there wasn't one damned thing that you could have done to prevent it.

That climber survived hacking off his arm and found people in proximity, so he lived through the ordeal. Suicide survivors can have that same experience.

Or not...the guilt heaped on a survivor about what that action would have done to their loved ones can make them feel like even more of a fuck-up than they did before. Neither the survivor nor his family can afford to indulge in what-ifs; everyone just has to keep surviving.

Does anyone ever state that all of the equipment and medication that can keep a body breathing when it's *trying* to die are the Devil's tools? No, they're 'Miracles' supposedly provided by God through modern science. Again, horse pucky. This goes back to my views on the Bible. If you're still reading, you won't be surprised to hear that I don't think God's rulings on either suicide or existing on tubes are known to anyone but himself and that, lacking that knowledge, you have the obligation to make your own best decision as to what's the right and moral thing for *you* to do for yourself or your loved one.

Some states have enacted 'Right to Die' laws and that's a step toward freedom to choose, but none of those laws give you the right to call Dr. Kevorkian because you've decided that you cannot face life without your penis, hearing, breast, vision, or whatever has become your personal last straw. No, you have to have some combination of doctors and legislators agree that you have only 'X' amount of time to live anyway, so if you want to check out earlier, they'll give you permission and means. That's not good enough. I want the right to quit when *I've* handled all I can without having to resort to the uncertainty of a cobbled together mix of whatever pills are in the house or making a horrifying mess for someone I love to find and clean up.

Senility takes a while to become obvious; cancer and any number of maladies that don't require external aids don't show for a time. Many of us can *look* like we're doing just great while we have some affliction of old age that impacts us more than we let on. We all need to be kind.

Speaking of senility, I'm no kind of health expert and am not presenting this as advice, so check with your doctor, your swami or the internet before you try it. Vitamin B-12 is a very accessible supplement that seems to address a lot of the issues of old age such as dementia, nerve degeneration, stroke, cognitive issues and depression. We'd have been better off to begin taking it in our 40's (are you listening, Millennials?), but if you get the go-ahead, give it a try.

Leslie Baker

The previous chapter was on finances in old age, this one on health; there are many things that link the two. There are lots of nutty ways to spend money just to squeeze out a few more miserable years. If they're *fabulous* years, that's different, but to just be bobbing from one health disaster to the next isn't my idea of a life well lived. We were never meant to live so long!

Advice: And speaking of sexy underwear, here's a tip from my birth mother that's the best advice she ever gave me. If young women are still using panty-liners for those iffy days, keep the opened box in your underwear drawer. You'll be amazed at how this speeds up your morning routine. Of course, you'll have to disregard this if you're wearing Depends these days; your drawers aren't big enough for your drawers!

...7...SENIOR JOY

So much of this book has to do with depressing topics and I promised at the beginning that I wouldn't blow smoke up your ass, but life without joy would be dreadful so let's take a moment to explore the topic. Remember former President G.H.W. Bush's words: "Old guys can still do stuff!"

Many of the things that have given us satisfaction, fun or meaning in our lives are harder to do as we age. Some things are so depressing for us to have to do *differently* that we opt to not do them at all. Fishing in a boat or along a craggy shore may not be safe for you anymore, which is certainly a piss-off, but you might be able to take some child in your life to one of those pay-per-catch town lakes and help her learn to bait a hook and fish. Sure, it's different, but you're giving your time and experience to a kid who will benefit from and remember the attention.

If you're lucky enough to be able to afford travel but can no longer handle long flights, look into bus tours to areas you've missed in our country. The couple of these trips I've taken (both to accompany someone I cared about) were surprisingly fun! If you'd told me beforehand that I'd consider riding a bus of my own volition, I'd have said you were nuts, but I'll definitely take another bus tour at some stage; the ones I took for other people were well organized and so easy on the travelers! The drivers were like having a combination tour-guide and bellhop at your fingertips.

Phillip and I try to take at least a couple of long driving trips a year while we still can and those trips light up our lives. Long after they're over, we derive immense pleasure from reviewing our photo albums and reliving our trips.

Now *there's* an old-fashioned source of pleasure that few people indulge in anymore. Photo albums are such a fulfilling, tactile way to treat yourself! We use our phones for taking gillions of photos, transfer them to our desktop computers for sorting and editing then email them to Walgreens for printing. Especially if you look on their site for the sale codes, having photos printed at any of the places that do it is so much cheaper and more professional than buying ink, paper and printing them yourselves. And the prints are ready for pick-up before we can get to town to do so. We buy a 3-ring binder for each year and photo pages online in boxes of 100. This is great fun for us and we've been surprised at how many people have mentioned how much more enjoyable it is to thumb through one of these albums than to scroll through someone's device to see photos.

Yesterday's News... The Tractor

I never want to live in a place where I don't run the risk of occasionally getting stuck behind a farm tractor for a mile or two of highway.

Being brought down to 15MPH while on your way to something 'important' is a great way to force yourself to take a deep breath and spend those few extra minutes thinking about what's REALLY important. And one of my most important quality-of-life gauges is that it be a rural life.

I feel so lucky to live in the place that's the home of most of my very best childhood memories. Although I'm sometimes brought to tears at the loss of a building that's even older than I am or the widening of a road that I remember as a dirt track, I am schooling myself to try to accept the fact that change, like other unpleasantness, happens.

We were visiting recently with some friends from Taylor who, like us, are always thinking that they're going to pick up and move to that place with the greener grass. The older we all get, though, the harder this place is to beat was the general consensus. That may have been an easier sell sitting outside at 75 degrees, sipping cocktails in the shade, surrounded by summer's colorful bounty than had it been 10 degrees and time to shovel snow.

But I've never minded even our harshest winters. We have such polite snow! It doesn't hang around for months on end becoming a gloppy, disgusting mess the way it does in wetter climates. You get the childlike joy of "Snow! Yay!" and the next day it's bright and sunny and mostly gone. This last winter was the first time in three years that we've had to have the driveway plowed; that's not a bad record.

Of course, being retired (of which I'm not a big fan) does give you the choice of staying in for a couple of days of 'bad' weather. I once lived and worked where you had to keep the block heater on your car plugged in 24/7 during several months of the year. If you didn't have that option, you had to go out every little while to start and let it run for a bit. Heavy equipment was never shut down except for maintenance, they just ran shifts and kept it running; heck, it was dark almost around the clock anyway, so why not? To go grocery shopping, you had to have an extra set of keys so that you could leave the car running and still lock it; all of those running cars caused dense ice fog to form over the town. No, I consider ours a pretty mild climate!

Friends from Florida were visiting here in June. They are people who enjoy every minute of living in a big, busy city complete with alligators in the residential areas. Not my cup of tea, but I was impressed with how much they love and take advantage of all their area offers. Those of us who can choose where to live are truly blessed.

———————

One of the things I treat myself to is an Ancestry subscription; I joined practically the day they went online. Genealogy is a great way to wile away (way too much) time, make use of and share all those boxes of old family stories and photos and to leave something that your grandkids might find interesting some day.

Please keep or rediscover the joy in your life, even if you have to jigger it to fit your new limitations or find a whole new source of enjoyment. You will not be the person you want to be if you don't have some interests to keep your mind engaged. If your mobility is so limited that you're stuck in a recliner a lot of the time, try to find some game on your laptop that gets you more engaged than just staring, slack-jawed, at the television. Take up knitting (hey, if it was manly enough for Rosey Grier...) or something else with simple tools that won't keep you struggling up for a sponge. Maybe join an on-line book club so you can have discussions on topics that interest you.

It's hard to do things on a lesser scale than you're used to. We have a large yard that has always been a major source of joy for us. Having to keep drawing in the boundaries of what we can reasonably keep landscaped anymore is just infuriating. Phillip and I have always not only enjoyed the yard for itself and the activity it's afforded us, but have been so proud when people oohed and aahed over it. More than once (even as I write this!) I've teared-up over the diminishment of what's possible for us to maintain. We'd be smart to sell the place and move into a retirement village while we're still strong and sentient enough to do so on our own, but every time we discuss doing so, we end up saying, to hell with it, we love it here and if we have to be hauled off in wheelbarrows, so be it. I apologize in advance to my son for not making the transition easier on *him* when he has to hoist that handcart.

Advice...Lowered expectations just come with the territory called old age and it's a challenge to find ways to deal with them without becoming bitter. Finding the joy was easier twenty years ago, but we still need it! A new or re-defined hobby is essential to our mental health; so, please, as long as you're able, make the effort. It's a gift you give yourself. Millennials, you can help your folks by encouraging new interests!

Leslie Baker

...8...FRIENDS & FAMILY

You know you've hit 'that time of life' when you begin to rummage around for a card for a friend but you're fresh out of sympathy and get well cards; you buy them by the gross and *still* can't keep up with the demand!

One of the saddest and most inescapable facts of aging is watching our contemporaries do it, too. We *expect* to see it in our parents; but as they die off and leave us as the family elders, we watch our siblings and friends, maybe those from kindergarten on, mirror our own battles with demon age. It becomes easy to get impatient with the new weaknesses and foibles they display. We wonder if Sam was always such a grouch, forgetting that he's dealing with health issues that he tries to keep under wraps. Or why Ruth has become an airhead, not having heard yet about the Dementia diagnosis. Even knowing that *we've* decided not to fish anymore because we can't trust our shaky old legs to get us in and out of the boat safely doesn't give us as much insight as might be hoped into what our nearest and dearest are dealing with.

The older we get, the more frequently we get the news that a friend's biopsy came back bad or that another friend has decided to forego further treatment. Every one of those calls is a twist of the knife; our hearts break for our friends and their loved ones, but we also feel the icy grip of foreboding for ourselves and whoever's next. You can't help the feeling of vulnerability; that the target on your back is getting bigger and bigger.

We all dread that late night phone call or a text delivered at midnight saying "call me first thing in the morning." Except for the arrival of a new grandchild, there is *no* good news that's going to come from either of those. As we get older, the damned things (late night calls, not grandchildren) come more often for a while and then, if you live long enough, they quit coming. Lordy, what a lose/lose proposition.

Many of us have children whose lives we worry that we'll adversely impact by our getting old and feeble. Yes, it's the time honored tradition to take care of your parents as they age, but most of us want to be independent for as long as possible and the idea of having to rely on our kids to parent us is hugely unappealing. While we might remember an aged relative being cared for in Grandmother's house, most of those old folks didn't live for too long once they became unable to live on their own. Now, with all of the 'miraculous' medications and implements available, we can be kept alive almost indefinitely. Is that to *anyone's* advantage?

That's not just a snark; I'm still waiting for someone to make an argument in favor of doing so that I'd buy. If *you*, personally, feel that it's beneficial to you or your loved ones to spend a ton of money to keep you technically alive, if that's your idea of life or fulfills your obligation to God, then that's what you need to do. That's *my* idea of Hell on Earth and I will (eventually!) *haunt* anyone who would make such a decision on my behalf!

I have known many people, some near and dear to me, who have a whole different take on this, though. They've felt, when the time came to make the decision to treat an incurable illness or to let it run it's course, that whatever time they could squeeze out of life with treatment was a precious gift and worth any cost in pain or dollars. I respect that right to choose, I really do. Keeping my mouth shut is not my strong suit, but I try hard in these cases to do so.

I have quite a few childless friends and I feel fully confident that all of them have made plans for their own end-of-life care and disposal. Why do I feel that others of us *with* children haven't been as conscientious about wills and estate plans? Do those of us with children have a subconscious feeling that there's a safety net there? The childless among us may have done stints care-taking our own parents, but that was a finite commitment, unlike that of parenthood. Maybe because they have always had such control over their own lives, without the chaos that a houseful of small, growing and teenage children can bring, non-parents realized early on that they needed to be diligent in making end of life plans. I find this contrast between parents and the childless to be a peculiar dichotomy.

Yesterday's News... Confederate Monuments I

How many of you have ever bought, sold, or been slaves? Neither have I.

So, since the vast majority of us likely answered "Not I" to that question, can we try to put this whole issue of tearing down Confederate monuments in perspective?

The criteria for this destruction seems to be that the person or organization represented by the statue espoused slavery and/or was a slave owner.

Where does this end? It's only a beginning to look at the crusade of the Mayor of Phoenix to eliminate "Robert E. Lee Street". What about Washington, Jefferson,

Madison, Monroe, Jackson, Van Buren, Harrison, Tyler, Polk, Taylor, Johnson and Grant? All of those Presidents owned slaves either while in or out of office. What is the proposal, here? We're going to allow the renaming of every street, town, historic home, city, school and hospital in the country that bears one of these names?! Don't be stupid.

But if we're <u>determined</u> to be stupid, why stop there? What about the coliseums in Europe? The Taj Mahal? The pyramids in Mexico and Egypt? Do you doubt that these wonders were built with slave labor? Or that they were built to glorify the owners of those slaves? Slavery is as old as civilization.

Are we going to bulldoze everything the world over that has a connection with it?

How about if we just don't buy, sell or become slaves and educate our children and ourselves on why it's a hideous practice? This ongoing self-flagellation over slavery by all of us who have NO connection to it has gotten completely out of hand. It's one more example of the tyranny of the minority. In using the term 'minority' I'm not referring to blacks. I suspect that well-grounded people, black <u>or</u> white, are not the ones tearing open old scars that are trying to heal. Ungrounded whites have bought into the crazy idea that we have some residual *guilt that we must atone for (or that slavery really <u>was</u> a good idea) while ungrounded blacks seem determined to burden their children with hates and resentments that shouldn't impact their lives.*

This is our (and the world's) history. We don't have to approve of every aspect of it to acknowledge it, but it is essential to <u>know</u> what our history is. Tearing down monuments to people who don't mesh with the current zeitgeist is akin to Hitler's burning of books. You don't like those ideas or practices? Easy-peasy, let's just destroy any evidence that they ever existed and do the Three Monkeys routine as we go on our merry way.

Please don't land all over me for not recognizing the failure of Reconstruction, the impact of Jim Crow laws, etc. Anyone coming of age in the '60's, even in an Arizona farm town, knew more than they wanted to about racial injustice. There will always be wacky, dangerous fringe groups on all sides espousing radical ideas, but I don't want to see the landscape of the world obliterated in the name of someone else's imagined guilt.

———

Have you ever noticed how age gaps between friends seem to become issues as we get older? Earlier, I mentioned some of the ways in which technology is harder the older we get and how that can impact our friendships. At 40, I had close friends in their 30's and others in their 50's. A gap of ten years was so insignificant that it was barely felt. Now, at 70, I've been noticing how people only 4 or 5 years younger than I seem more adaptable to ever-changing mores, have more energy and more 'normal' eating & entertaining habits. It's just the opposite with friends the tiniest bit older; the gaps seem disproportionately wide. It (like so many aspects of aging) is a return to childhood; you relate best to people very close to your own age, you eat nasty pabulum, you have no hair, you wear diapers and bibs and are becoming more and more dependent on having someone push you around in a wheeled device.

Many of us really aren't interested in making new friends because we've learned that being a good friend is a real commitment and we just don't have it in us to further our obligations. Acquaintances are a fine and pleasant part of life, but friends require nurturing and only the best are ultimately worth the effort. As people in our circles withdraw or die, it's one more area in which we notice aloneness, whether purposeful or not.

The folks who make it their business to care for oldsters are particularly attuned to the downside of isolation; all sorts of seemingly unrelated things are attributed to it. And yet, isolation can feel so undemanding!

A friend who was widowed five years ago had been taking a bumpy ride downhill since then. Anna has a bucket of money and had always been very active until blindness curtailed her activities. After the death of her husband, Anna had hired various part- or full-time drivers and helpers, but had become increasingly bitter, isolated and unwell. Finally, her kids stepped in and insisted that she could no longer live in that big house away from any of them and helped her to find a (*way* upscale!) care facility near one of them. Well! Anna's transformation has been glorious! She is back in a highly socialized milieu and is thriving in it. She doesn't have to drive to find a bridge game or a cocktail. There's a shuttle to Saks with a nice driver to load all those bags. And there's always conversation (or peace and quiet) to be had. The re-bloom of this vivacious woman has made me rethink my long held and negative perceptions of 'A Place for Pop' type facilities.

No one wants to be carted off to one of those smelly, depressing places where oldsters are wheeled into the hallways to molder in their dirty diapers. And most of us don't have the funds for a top-flight place like Anna was able to afford. But if there's a viable alternative to those two choices, I've seen for the first time how a person can truly benefit from having full-time care, no homeowner worries and an active social life all under one roof. Until this experience, I would never in a million years have considered such a lifestyle for myself. Now, after having just replaced windows, repainted the house and fought all day yesterday with our irrigation system, it doesn't look all that bad!

If you and your parents are looking for anything from a 6-bed 'group home' to an $8K-a-month 'senior living' facility, keep a couple of things in mind. Don't go on tour or visiting day; drop in unannounced a time or two and see as much as you can before they boot you. Lunchtime is a good time to do this; you can see how people socialize and are fed then. If you're looking at a place with several 'levels' of care, be sure that Memory Care is one of them. I've known of too many people whose parents went into a place with all their marbles but later developed dementia of one sort or another and had to be moved to a different facility. That's a traumatic move for the patient *and* her family. Memory Care is a certification that not all places have or will get even if they tell you that the application is 'in process.'

The whole ordeal of deciding that it's time for a home, choosing one and paring down for the move is a hard one. Get the best advice you can and try not to be in a huge hurry.

Advice: Do <u>not</u> move to someplace you've never been because your son is moving there and taking your grandchildren with him.   And, Millennials: discourage such a move by your parents for <u>many</u> reasons! We knew of a couple who completely uprooted themselves in their 60's due to a son's job transfer. Nine months later the son's family decided that they hated Iowa and were moving to New Mexico. Our friends hated Iowa too, but they didn't have the physical or monetary wherewithal to move anywhere else. It ruined their lives.

...9...DEATH, DATING and SEX

Being widowed is a topic that deserves it's own chapter; I'm not the person to write it, but right now, I'm all you've got. My former husbands have all escaped before I could kill them, so neither widowhood nor prison have been in my experience. Having watched friends, family and Hospice clients begin to rebuild their lives after loss has taught me only a few things that I'd hope to remember if I found myself in that situation. (Which I won't; even though Phillip is 18 years older than I am, he's gonna outlive us all!).

The most immediate thought I'd offer someone who's just buried or scattered a spouse is to wait for a full year before you make *any* major decisions. Certainly there are exceptions if the death is the end of a multi-year ordeal that has allowed the survivor to make plans gradually and rationally while helping the spouse to get through it. But if you've 'only' had to deal with the situation for a couple of years, you've probably been so intensely involved in the everyday commitments entailed that you haven't had much clear-headed time to yourself to plan ahead.

I've known of people who, after sending all of their loved one's clothes to Goodwill soon after the death, have been sorry. They or the kids have remembered a favorite scarf or hat that would have been a beloved keepsake. The same is true of his books or her china. Unless there's a compelling reason to 'get rid of it all,' just let it perk for a year. Go ahead and box it up (well labeled) if you really want to tidy up, and if, at the end of a year, you haven't wanted to salvage something, calmly let it go.

Again, without true urgency to do so, don't sell your home, take in a roommate, get a pet, spend money painting the house or doing anything else that can't be undone. You will have times of clarity when you feel capable of and even anxious to 'start over' but they'll probably come and go.

Let yourself get through that awful year of 'Firsts' before you try to tackle life again. Take some short trips, try a new hobby; the sort of thing that isn't a major commitment. But the first time you face his birthday, your anniversary, Christmas, etc. will be hard, don't add to that by having huge lifestyle changes going on, too.

Yesterday's News - Mary's Letter

One of the things I love about the local paper is the Letters to the Editor section. While some writers become a little too familiar, it's usually fun to see a name you recognize.

I recently saw a signature that made me smile. 'Mary' is a woman with whom I shared the care and loss of a mutually dear friend a few years ago. We found that we had little in common except our love and concern for our dying friend, but we enjoyed each other's company and helped each other through a difficult time. I'll always think fondly of her.

Mary and I always knew that we were on totally different sides of the political aisle and carefully avoided that topic. I got to know her as a woman who cares for her community by volunteering and is very obviously crazy about her family and her pets. She's an immensely strong and talented woman whose art just blows me away.

After reading Mary's letter to the editor, her despairing thoughts on a hot political topic made me reflect on my reaction to her words. Had I not known her to be the wonderful person she is, I might have read her letter, rolled my eyes and dismissed the unknown writer as a *left-wing-nut or something equally (from <u>my</u> point of view) disparaging.*

Instead, I found that, while I strongly disagreed with her views, I didn't feel anger or condescension, but hoped that Mary would be able to focus her energies elsewhere. I wish her contentment.

Wouldn't it be nice if we could feel as magnanimous toward at least most of the people on the other side of political issues? To cut them some slack because we know them to be good people with whom we sometimes disagree?

To stay friends with those with whom we strongly disagree on one subject, I think you have to know them well enough to appreciate and honor the (kind, funny, compassionate or whatever) aspects of them drew you together in the first place. If the acquaintance is short or limited to a specific interest (say, painting class or quilting) we probably shouldn't presume to criticize or try to change their opinion.

As I've pondered my reaction to Mary's letter, I've vowed to try being a little less quick to hurl invective toward letter writers whose signature I don't recognize and, instead, to take a deep breath and try to react as though their opinions are those of a friend.

That's going to be a tough call! I find venting my spleen to be invigorating. But it's good to have goals, right?

Getting a pet is something many see as a way to fill the quiet in their lives. If you've always had pets until recently, then you know what it entails; just remember that you will be the only one doing all of the walking, grooming and cleaning up; your partner's absence will be felt in many little ways that will surprise you. When you laugh at some silly thing your pet does, you'll be saddened that your partner isn't sharing the amusement with you. If this will be your first pet, talk with friends about the down as well as the upsides of pet ownership.

When getting a dog later in life, get a small one. Even if you hate the little yappers. I've known of two different couples recently who were trying to cope with their own health issues *and* those of their elderly, large dogs. The dog required help into the car to go to vet or groomer and neither person in the couple had the strength to boost him even when, in one case, it was to be the final trip for the poor old dog. One couple had invested in a ramp designed to help a dog in and out of their small SUV. For a year, it did help, but then the old fellow got so blind and deaf that his balance was way off and he became afraid of the ramp. I get it, I've always had big dogs, but I won't again.

If you think that adding a pet to your life is fraught with issues, imagine adding a *person*! I used to think that the best compliment you could give your dead spouse was to remarry. If your marriage was so happy that you'd do it all again, what could be a better tribute to him/her? Well, yes, but...

We've all known of people who got married soon after the loss of a spouse and it's hard to walk the line between being *happy for* and *worried for* them. If both of the happy couple are widows who have known each other for years (maybe as part of a bridge foursome with their deceased partners) I'd be thrilled for them, but there are a lot of ways for this to go south and the lovebirds need to recognize that their friends and family aren't just being party-poops but are genuinely concerned for their well-being. On the other hand, we don't have a lot of time left at this stage and if you've found a partner you really feel comfortable with, go for it. Don't let stifling traditions about waiting a year or kids who think it's disrespectful to their dead parent make the choice for you. If you aren't capable of making this decision for yourself, someone will come along and take you to a home soon, anyway, so make hay....

Whatever you ultimately decide about dating, marrying or cohabiting, please don't make steps toward it in that first year (again, with the caveats noted above.) Of all of the decisions you'll have to make as your life moves forward, this is the most crucial. Men and women get taken to the cleaners (and killed) every year by users who are ready to pounce on them at their most vulnerable.

Remember that you're a sitting duck; not only are you lonely, you're old. On-line dating, Classmates, the local bar, Craigslist; there are innumerable ways to connect with people and if you're extremely careful you might find a gem in there. But you're not prepared to be that careful soon after you've buried a spouse.

Probably the safest ways to meet people are in church or by volunteering in an area that *genuinely* interests you. And if you ease into a new interest without looking for 'dates,' you might be able to handle this within that first year. Just don't join the NRA because you think you'll find a manly man or your kinda gal there. Tutor young readers at the library; join a group who maintains hiking trails; take a class. I'd be cautious at this point in life about serving the underprivileged in soup kitchens, handing out coats and that sort of good work unless it's something that you've done for years. The people you'll come into contact with are needy and many of them are old hands at conning the vulnerable. Take care of yourself first.

If you later decide to try on-line dating, only 'meet' <u>*local*</u> people and insist on meeting in person in a public place in broad daylight *after the first two or three online contacts.* Don't let a face-to-face meeting be delayed beyond a week or ten days. I'm serious about this.

Involve your friends; make sure that someone either goes with you to a first meeting or knows where and when you're going. *Never, never, never* give anyone you haven't known for 50 years a plug nickel. Ever. For any reason. Ever. I know I'm being an un-fun shrew about this, but it's just shocking how many scammers (and worse) compile their dating wish lists through the obituaries.

Geriatric sex. Pfftt...Good luck with that one.

Advice: The very best way I've found to get the smell of fish, onions and the like out of my hands is to, before applying soap, lather up with old, original Noxzema. I always have a big blue jar of it under the kitchen sink.

...10...HOSPICE

As I write this, I have a childhood friend, the husband of another friend and the mother of a longtime friend who should *all* be on Hospice. I have encouraged the primary caregivers in those families to call Hospice themselves and ask for an evaluation because the family physicians won't bring it up. But facing death head-on is a helluva hard step to take.

In 1993, the reigning misperception was that Hospice care was primarily for AIDS patients. AIDS was in its heyday then, with many bugaboos working against it and those prejudices also worked against easy societal acceptance of Hospice care. A physician recently stated that too many people think that Hospice care is only for *cancer* patients. The common thread there is that many Hospice organizations haven't gotten any better in all these years at clarifying their mission for the public.

Hospice today is a radically different organization than it was when I began volunteering for one over 25 years ago. I'm heartbroken and infuriated over the management practices currently imposed on physicians, care facilities and Hospice by the damned government. *However,* the management practices generally don't impact *you* as the user of the service.

The Hospice *philosophy* is a fabulous one. Simply put, Hospice recognizes that dying is a part of the normal life cycle and focuses on enhancing the quality of remaining life for the patient and his caregivers. Palliative (meaning to relieve pain without addressing the underlying condition) care minimizes discomfort and every effort is made to allow the patient to spend his last months in his own home.

The point is to catch the dying process <u>early</u>, give the caregiver the support she needs and to allow the patient to die comfortably in his own home without the charade that he is going get well. No more toughing it out through that hour or two before he can have the next scheduled pain pill. No more being nauseous from the cocktail of meds and the confusion of dealing with multiple (and often conflicting) instructions. Blessed relief is usually possible.

Everybody thinks they can handle the end-of-life care of their loved one by themselves and that there's some sort of valor in doing so. I don't think that God is going to dole out Brownie points for damned near killing yourself in trying to care for someone who desperately needs you to be strong when they can't be.

With Hospice, as long as a person has the mobility and *desire* to get out and have some fun, that's *encouraged.* Then, when the patient is no longer mobile or responsive, s/he is kept at home in a clean hospital bed and fresh nightclothes.

In my early years with Hospice when it was common practice for a client to have a Hospice team in place for six months or more, we volunteers were able to give our people some wonderful experiences before they were bedridden. One lovely lady had always meant to but had never visited the magnificent Monarch butterfly colony in our county. Her daughters were caring for her *and* their small children as well as working full time, so she hated to ask them to take her. I was thrilled to do so and the joy she received from that day still makes me smile; it was a real 'bucket list' moment even before that term existed! I was able to take a couple of different clients Christmas shopping for their loved ones and help them wrap what would not otherwise have been surprises for that last shared Christmas.

Those and so many more wonderful Hospice experiences happened because people were put on Hospice *early!*

Twenty-five years ago, it was very rare to have a client who ended up dumped into a facility at the end of their life, now it seems to be the norm. I don't remember *ever* (until recently) having had a caregiver who was reduced to desperation over the care of their loved one. I remember the calm, quiet efficiency of a Hospice staff that prioritized the patient and the caregiver equally and did not let either of them see any of the juggling and re-evaluations of their situation that were going on behind the scenes.

Now, it's no wonder caregivers are giving up and allowing (or begging for) their loved ones to be 'placed' in a facility while on Hospice home care. This is a direct result of Hospice not being called in early enough *and* of continuing medications long beyond their usefulness. End-stage personal care for a dying patient can be a huge burden, both physically and emotionally, for their primary caregivers who are often elderly and/or fragile themselves.

When both the patient and the caregiver have been instructed by a doctor that a patient be dressed, hauled and hoisted around the house all day, plopped in a chair, dragged back and forth to the john and into town for doctor's appointments, there is *nothing* peaceful about that for either of them! No wonder the caregiver is beaten down to the point where a facility for the patient is the only answer. This scenario is precisely what

Hospice was meant to ease. When all of his ailments are still being 'managed' by medications, the dying process can take much longer and be much worse than it needs to be for both patient and caregiver.

The importance of respite care for caregivers is hard to overstate. Caregiver burnout is one of the *worst* results of not being told soon enough what you're actually dealing with and of having to go through the motions indicating a person is going to recover.

Asinine 'Elder Abuse' regulations, while well intentioned, have made the care of Hospice patients even more onerous by taking away commonsense aids to care. To say that it's 'abuse' to put up the bedrails for a patient who is in danger of wandering and/or falling is just clueless in any world except that of government regulation.

Here's where my version of 'Just Say No' comes in. Adhering to laws that impact major portions of their income hamstrings your doctors and most Hospice organizations. *You* are not impacted by those laws. *You* do not have to go to doctor's appointments or take medications that you deem meaningless to your dying process. You can just say no. Whether you are on Palliative Care (typically for diagnoses of somewhat longer than 6 months to live) through a Hospice organization or on actual Hospice Care (usually a diagnosis of 6 months or less to live), you have been diagnosed with a life-limiting condition. Be your own best advocate in deciding how those +/- six months will be spent.

Doctors are not God and cannot force you to take one more pill than you agree to take or go to one more nonsensical appointment. In this regulatory environment, the patient and his caregivers *have* to advocate for themselves.

If the time comes that *you're* the one with the terminal diagnosis, I hope that you'll encourage or insist that your spouse or other primary caregiver call Hospice. While you still have all your marbles, do a realistic assessment of what a huge burden your loved one will be shouldering. They are no doubt more than willing to do so but may not be as willing to acknowledge their own limitations. Give them your permission to ask for help as early as possible; it could be a long haul for you both.

The individuals who align themselves with Hospice organizations are, in my experience, fabulous people. They have great resources and do their very best for their clients. The regulatory morass is a nightmare for them and impacts the quality of care that they're trying to deliver, but they hang in because they believe in what they're doing and try very hard to not let the behind-the-scenes chaos disrupt the quiet and calm that they're bringing to their patients.

Hospice is, with all it's issues, still a much better option for end-of-life care than _no_ Hospice. If you suspect that you're entering the last phase of your life, but your doctor won't have The Talk, nothing keeps _you_ from calling Hospice and asking for an evaluation. Hospice has (the world's best) nurses who will be in to monitor the patient's progress and be vigilant in keeping pain at bay. Wonderful people will come in to help the patient with bathing and other personal needs. When requested, spiritual advisors are available to help the patient and the family to navigate this new territory called 'dying.' Trained Hospice volunteers will come in and visit, read to or just be there quietly with the patient while the caregiver goes out to do some errands or get some vital 'me' time.

A practical word to a family using Hospice: If you're the caregiver, please don't be afraid of the Morphine in the fridge when you get to that stage. The nurse wouldn't have left it for you if she didn't trust you to use it. No one's going to think that you're trying to kill your loved one (unless you _are_, in which case, you need different help than I can offer) or taking the 'easy' way of handling him for your _own_ relief. 'Pain' covers a lot; a patient's psychic, mental and physical distresses are all 'pain'. If you're not sure when to use the Morphine, talk with any of the Hospice people who come into your home. They'll get you the answer if they don't have it.

You, the caregiver, are not *bothering* anyone by calling Hospice or doing the *right* thing by trying to handle it all yourself. You're the reason Hospice exists! This is a gift you can give yourself and your loved one early in the process. The quality of life for every family member is improved when a good Hospice group is asked into your lives.

The enriching nature of Hospice relationships is evidenced by the fact that many people have come into Hospice, either as a volunteer or in a career move, because they've experienced the service firsthand, want to be a part of it and give back the support they received during a difficult time. These are people who've walked the path you're on and want to light the way for you; please let them be there for you when the time comes.

Advice: Never swerve. This could be but isn't a metaphor for something. It's serious advice. When driving at speed, do not swerve to avoid <u>anything</u> that isn't human. Not dog, deer or houseboat. The mother of one of my son's kindergarten friends was driving home along a rural, two-lane highway from a college night class some miles away.

She swerved to avoid a skunk and ended up in the ditch. She was paralyzed from the neck down for the rest of her eight or ten years. Whatever it is, hit that sonofabitch and take your chances.

...II...GATES

"**W**ait...aren't you the one who spent years flippantly saying that you couldn't believe in a God who had no sense of humor? Or who had a thin skin?" came the voice.

"Yes, that's me" you answer, confident that St. Peter is preparing to wave you right through those magnificent Pearly Gates on this glorious, light-filled morning.

Your God was too busy with important things to take major offense at swearing, right? He wouldn't have given you the ability to enjoy ice cream, sex and horse-racing if he was going to damn you *for* enjoying them, wasn't that your reasoning?

Pete steps from behind his imposing podium as sudden thunderclouds and lightning produce a deafening, blinding maelstrom that envelops you both. His face has gone dark and wrathful, his fingers are flashing bolts of energy. Robes whipping furiously around him, eyes so fierce you can't meet them, he roars in a voice that overwhelms the storm: "You imbecile!! Who did you think you were *dealing* with?! Who did you think those commandments were directed at if not at *your* prideful, sinning, insignificant self?!"

"But...but..." you sputter, ducking your head and hunching your shoulders to avoid a blast from the storm.

"Nothing!! *Not one word* from your sniveling mouth!" Peter bellows. "God Almighty will hear your mewling excuses and you will know the *meaning* of fury!"

You've gone through life grateful to a God whose requirements of you so nicely conformed to the parameters by which you chose to live it. He has expected you to be respectful of others, generous to those less fortunate than you, kind to all living things and other guidelines that really haven't proven to be too onerous.

And now *this*?! Sheesh, how much worse could Hell be than this onslaught of wrath from both nature and a fellow whose state of being is unclear. Is he human? Divine? And...wait!...what is he doing _now_?! Good God in Heaven! He's become a whirling dervish that seems to envelop all of heaven, hell and earth. You're swirled into it like strawberries into a blender...the howl is horrific...and then it stops.

You're afraid to look up from your facedown sprawl on the ground...or whatever that surface is. Are you in one piece? If nothing else, the silence is blessed. And then it's broken by a voice you don't recognize..."Boy, he's a wild man, isn't he?" Your confidence long gone, you have no idea how to respond; is it even *you* being addressed? Is that a rhetorical question? Are there others included in the query? You reluctantly peep up to see an aura of calm, kind of a warm, undefined glow.

Raising your head higher, you see a guy who is the spitting image you've always held of God: long white hair and beard, intense eyes and billowing white robes.

"You can get up, things have calmed down" he says. The voice is surprisingly...human; not even very theatrical. What's the protocol here? Is this even God or another one of his unpredictable minions? Once on your feet, should you bow? Grovel? This is uncharted territory.

Trying, as you rise, to straighten the 'Sunday Best' garb you were buried in, you're asked to take a seat. The two of you appear to be in a huge, storybook garden with inviting benches under sun-dappled trees. The place is comfortably shabby, not manicured to perfection but fully delightful. Choosing a metal armchair with peeling turquoise paint, you sit and wonder.

"So...Saint Peter tells me that you have an attitude" the man (or whatever) says conversationally. "Now, don't get *defensive* about that, I'm just trying to figure out what to do with you. You seem to have lived a pretty decent life," he mused as he scanned some notes on a yellow pad. "None of the automatic disqualifiers here, but no mind boggling heroics, either. Not that those are required; I realize that life is like running a gauntlet just to be decent. But why don't you tell me what makes you think that I'm not a stickler for adherence to religious guidelines?"

"Um, well, Sir...gosh, I'm so nervous. I don't want to be a smart aleck, but I'd have to ask which denomination you're referring to?"

The silence is benign but unbroken.

"Religion always just confused me, Sir. There are so many of them and most don't agree on much. Some churches rewrite their texts because they don't agree with each *other* on what the Bible actually says or means. It doesn't seem like it should be that complicated, if you see what I mean."

Left to flounder in the stillness, you try another tack. "Did you actually tell those people what to write in the Bible? Did the Commandments really appear on Earth? Is Jesus really your son, or is he a human manifestation of *you?*" After each question, there's been no response, so you just keep digging the hole deeper.

"Faith seemed so much simpler when I was a kid; my parents told me that God expects this or that and so do we. It was basic: be kind, do well and pay your own way. I haven't always nailed it, but my life has been happier and less complicated when I did.

I really apologize if I made you feel disrespected by not adhering to any one religion's criteria; insulting you was never my intention, Sir."

The big guy replies: "If you *are* admitted to Heaven, what are your dreams and expectations?"

"Oh. Wow. Well, I guess the thing that I hope for the very most is to be reunited, in whatever form you choose, Sir, with all of the loved ones from my life. To let them know how much I've missed and loved them every day and how important they were to me. I was careless in so many cases about letting them know that when I had the chance."

After a long pause and receiving a searing once-over, you begin to think that your goose is cooked. You imagine having that funeral attire licked off your body by the flames of Hell. You mourn the loss of your loved ones all over again. You wonder what you could have done to better show your love of and respect for God.

Then...Poof! God is gone and so are your clothes. The light blinds you for a moment before you begin to see the magical garden populate with the auras of all of your favorite people, pets and experiences. They're all full of love for you and joy at your arrival.

There is a God. There is a Heaven. Glory Hallelujah!

...12...THE UPSIDE

Fooled you. There *is* no upside to getting old. Of course we always hear that it beats the alternative, and on the days when you wake up feeling like a million bucks, it's easy to agree; but what about those days that keep getting closer and closer together when every single thing is so difficult, painful or humiliating that you feel like you've been inadvertently entered into some cruel marathon?

We had a rollicking lunch the other day with some friends who told us that they'd just ordered their headstone. Like us, they're in remarkably good shape and very active for their ages and we all howled at the thought of parking that stone out behind the garage until it's needed.

I've often thought that the people who completely lose touch with reality are the lucky ones because they aren't aware, finally, of the state they're in. It's hell for the people *around* them, certainly, but to be blissfully unaware isn't nearly as bad as knowing exactly what a living corpse you've become and having lost all ability to do one damned thing about it. Our miracles of modern medicine keep people alive who are reduced to begging with their eyes to be released.

Advance Directives and Pre-Planning are a part of all of our lives at this stage. Which is good, because if we leave it all up to others, we might end up in a mayonnaise jar on the back porch.

There's just no end to it...until there is.

...13...AAAHH...MILLENNIALS

I f you're under 40 and made it through any of the preceding, I salute you! You're not the only one who isn't even remotely interested in the travails of old age; we oldsters find it pretty damned boring, too. My wish for you is that you make the very most of and be grateful for every day. When you get to be fifty, start gobbling life with a spoon because the years from fifty to seventy are Prime Time!

Yesterday's News...Money for Nuthin'

Big article in the Republic recently regarding the 'Millennial' generation's being significantly less affluent than their parents, the Boomers. The illustration was of a tall tree; lush and full on one side and looking like it had a severe bark-beetle infestation on the other.

When we Boomers were raising our kids, what was the National Debt? What was the percentage of people on the dole? How many people felt that they should still be on their parent's health insurance policies at age 26? How many people viewed six years in college studying The

Effect of Origami on Bi-Sexual Muskrats as time and money well spent?

We're fast approaching the moment when we have more people collecting money from the government than we have people paying taxes into it. When that tipping point is reached, we're sunk. If I'm only working and paying taxes so that my neighbor can live on those taxes, where's my motivation to contribute? Why not just join him in the money line?

We paid into Social Security and Medicare all of our working lives with the expectation that they'd offer us a cushion in our dotage. They were never meant to provide a lavish retirement income or all of our healthcare expenses, but to keep us from penury. They're a good idea because too many of us, given the temptations of a new boat or bigger house lack the restraint to save as much as we should. And those programs are at least partially funded by money we earned. (Regardless of the fact that one former President believed that we didn't build our own businesses, careers or, by extension, retirement funds. This was the same President who, in eight agonizingly long years, doubled the National Debt that every other president before him (combined!) had accumulated. A real rocket scientist, that one). No one currently over age 55 is expected to be affected by essential upcoming changes to Medicare and Social Security programs.

For those of you who are entranced by the idea of getting in on the same 'free' healthcare that your grandparents have through Medicare, allow me to point out that, not only did they contribute to those plans while working, but in most cases they still have somewhere in the neighborhood of $135. deducted monthly from their gross check to keep paying for their healthcare. NOT 'free.' Also not 'free' are medical benefits through pension plans; depending on the plan, an amount is deducted from the gross every month for any health insurance they provide. NOT 'free.'

'Free' (as in: health-care, college, child-care, etc.) is an illusion. Nothing is free. Someone's picking up the tab. As Margaret Thatcher famously said, "Socialism is fine until you run out of other people's money". This country has plunged into the fairy-tale of Socialism (aka: 'Progressivism') while shunning only the actual word. At least Bernie Sanders has the stones to embrace the word.

I'm not surprised at the news that our kids are in worse shape than we were at their ages. There's only so much money to go around and when you have a government that spends like a drunken uncle, the impact is going to be felt by us all.

Leslie Baker

Believe it or not, most of us old crones don't *feel* old. You can look at us and see your Grandmother, boss or Wal-Mart cart tender; we're crooked, wrinkled and bent; have funny or no hair, wear goofy clothes and eat crappy food. But once we walk away from the morning mirror after getting our dentures secured and our remaining hair sprayed firmly into place, we feel *your* age. Until we're brought up short by pain that won't subside, the death of yet another friend or some of the damned technology that comes so easily to you, we don't *feel* old.

But we don't understand you. In any ten-year span, the world you live in changes many times faster than it did when we were young. Technology has changed not just *things*, but attitudes, morals and values at lightning speed. From the time that we oldsters were born until we reached our fifties, the telephone and typewriter really didn't change very much. From your birth to today, think of all the iterations *you've* seen in just those two examples.

The following observations, although they may be harsh at times, aren't meant as condemnations as much as they're meant to offer you a peek at how some of the elders in your own life see things. There's nothing evenhanded here, they're my opinions, so please try to not be so offended that you can't pick out a few nuggets that do appeal.

Until you have grown children of your own, you'll not realize how much your parents have learned in all their years of living. Many of us don't ever get the chance to tell our parents that we're sorry for having been know-it-all little twits once that light bulb *does* fire up. If your parents are still alive (and deserving) throw them a bone while you still can and let them teach your adult self something. I promise that you'll be glad you did.

Advice: I'm repeating this one in case you missed it the first time; it may be the most important thing in the book... When your parent's or grandparent's birthdays roll around, make your call to them as early in the day as you think they'll be fully caffeinated. Don't wait til later. Your call will be the highlight of their day and they'll want to brag about and enjoy it all day.

...14...A LITTLE BACKGROUND

I'm over seventy and began school when girls still had to wear skirts to school and most other public venues. Women didn't usually work outside of the home unless they were...gasp!..old maids or...gasp & faint...divorced; when they *did* work, they were paid half a man's wages and couldn't say 'shit' if they had a shoe-full. Yet, I have never once in my life felt like a 'victim' and can't for the life of me see the attraction in labeling yourself as one. Advancements in 'equality' happen every single day if you advocate for yourself.

And, if you had suggested to my Gramma that claiming no *gender* could give her a better quality of life, she'd have called for the men in the white jackets (a term unfamiliar in this era when the insane are left on the streets in order to 'fulfill their potential'). This woman raised *me* to be a woman who could do any damned thing she pleased. I certainly haven't taken full advantage of all the opportunities offered to me but I've even more certainly never been a victim. My choices were mine as are the rewards and penalties. No, I've never been mistaken for

Mother Theresa, but I've always carried my own weight and the responsibility for my decisions.

...15...FEMINISM

W hile I don't remember ever having burned a bra, I *am* guilty of having gone joyfully without one during the wild and crazy '60's and '70's. Does that make me a feminist?

Does anyone even know *how* to define feminism these days? Women's rights (like those of everyone who isn't a fire hydrant) are certainly widely discussed and used as media fodder, but what are they?

If you know me or have read much of what I write, you already know that I take a pretty dim view of all this carrying on about 'rights.' Regardless of what the ACLU would have you believe, we all have unheard of rights in this country, many of them hard earned. Just because one's life hasn't been a bowl of cherries doesn't mean that you've been discriminated against or have had your *rights* denied. You might have suffered bad breaks or genuine disabilities that have, indeed, made your life harder than most, but I don't see that as a meal ticket for life in any but the most serious instances.

Our welfare system was enacted to offer a safety net to help those who had fallen on hard times until they could get back on their feet. I doubt that any of us begrudge helping the truly disabled or momentarily desperate, but that isn't how the system is being used today.

Due to abuse of that system by politicians trolling for votes by encouraging dependence on government handouts, we now have several generations of families who have never worked on the books. When most children wouldn't even have a clue what AFDC/TANF *means*, many young third generation recipients of our tax dollars have already learned to be crafty and deceitful in order to protect their family's livelihood. This entitled attitude has filtered into society until many now expect *everything* to be *given* to *everybody*. Whole new generations of voters, many needy families with dependent children have been enveloped by the progressives/socialists and *women* have been rolled into the mix of the oppressed. Women want equal pay for unequal work, free childcare and free birth control all to accommodate choices that they've made for themselves.

Yesterday's News... The Twilight Zone

We here on the hill had a couple of up-close and personal brushes with the future a year or two ago. Many of our banks and retail outlets lost the use of their computer systems when, first, some nut down in the valley dug up a fiber-optic cable then, another nut shot out a transformer somewhere on the reservation. That's not very sophisticated deviltry to have had the impact it did!

I remember feeling that I'd stumbled into the fifth dimension or a sorry sci-fi movie when everyone in the bank was standing around looking at each other and the tellers and realizing that none of our plastic or much else was working. Yes, we could get a (very) little cash if we were regular customers, but there was a super weird vibe in the place. A store I frequent had locked the doors and put up a sign saying, basically, that they didn't know what the hell was going on, but they were closed until it stopped.

Shortly after that, I got rid of my 2013 computer on wheels (still quaintly called a 'car') and got one a little older with fewer tech features and 100K more miles on it. I'd asked my brother (a major techie) how long it would be before our cars could be disabled remotely the way the local ATM's and cash registers had been. He said it was already technically possible but unlikely that it would become much of an issue anytime soon. You guys who have a '75 Ford rusting away out there behind the barn are the smart ones; just stock up on spark plugs while you can still get them.

In January, there was a story on a warning by Homeland Security regarding the 'Hacking' of people's defibrillators and/or pacemakers. Seriously? Yes. In a comforting statement, one of the laboratories involved noted that it was ".....not aware of deaths or injuries caused by the problem". And the manufacturer has made a software repair available. Now, doesn't that make you feel all warm and fuzzy?

I'm not kidding when I tell you that I feel like one of those lunatics wearing aluminum foil hats and waiting to be transported by the flying saucer version of Uber.

This is all without even addressing the issues of self-driving cars. Or of home devices that you can talk to through your smartphone and they'll start a roast at 350 degrees or finish painting the den. And those things are supremely hackable.

I have no solutions to offer. I did, however, download instructions for making a great tin foil hat and I'm going to get started on it right away.

———————

Many women seem to feel that men, just by being born male, are guilty of Male Toxicity. Let's have a little look at <u>Female</u> Toxicity, shall we? From the time they first climb on Daddy's lap to ask for a pony, to the day they flutter their eyelashes to get out of a speeding ticket, to the time they accept a date with a guy they aren't really interested in because he has tickets to the best box at a rodeo or a polo match, girls and women use men in every way possible. For this behavior, they're indulgently called 'flirts.' The worst of these women 'accidentally' get pregnant so a guy who otherwise wouldn't, will marry them (and if you think for an instant that that doesn't still happen, you're not paying attention.)

A hard-assed feminist who wants to trade the right to be female for the right to castigate men for being male, will need to choose her companions carefully and not be too surprised when nobody, male or female, actually likes her.

If buying into that nonsense is part of the new feminism, then you can definitely count me out.

Advice: Never be without your own money. Yes, I know that you got married for better or for worse to the love of your life. But so did every divorced person on the planet. Make sure that you always have a credit card <u>in your own name,</u> not just as a joint account. If you're in a high enough tax bracket, own a piece of real estate as "sole and separate" property. Have a bank account, however small,

with nobody's name on it but yours. Male or female, trust
me on this.

...16...EQUAL RIGHTS

Discrimination and bias on myriad issues are as old as dirt. That doesn't excuse them, but if you live in the real world, it's on you to figure out how to avoid them just like you avoid potholes and bad seafood. It isn't society's duty to legislate any but the most grievous instances of offense to your delicate little self. Certainly, men and women are hideously harmed in life but if you've been raised to believe that you have the strength to persevere and the responsibility to do so, most of us can carry on. The current zeal to make everything equal and perfect is a fool's errand.

What's perfect for *you* usually infringes on someone else's idea of perfection. What constitutes *equal* for you is an unjust inequality to the next guy. If you keep trying to get that table leveled by sawing off it's legs a little here and a little there, you're going to end up with something other than a table and, trust me, it's not going to be a level playing field. It's going to be a pack of pissed off victims with saws in their hands.

If you want to know about *discrimination*, try waddling in the shoes of a fat woman (of any color) for a while! I've had slim, beautiful years in my life and fat ones. The only visibility you have as a fat woman is as the (big) butt of jokes and as an object lesson in self-control for suburban moms to point out to their little lovelies. Yes, in most cases, you have the physical means to control your weight, but the psychological strength to do so can be hard to come by. Where do these women go for *their* equal rights?

Boys used to play war games while girls played with dolls. Except when they didn't. Kids of both genders have always shared in whatever games they were playing. I shot as many cap guns as did my brother and he liked my playhouse as much as I did (though he may have been more inclined to deem it a fort). But a few years ago women decided that they wanted to be, *had the right* to be on the front lines in real wars, not just the cap-gun variety. While that may look good on paper, it's less attractive when you consider that most enemy combatants aren't likely to be as evolved as these gals and would prefer to capture and gang-rape women rather than men. If my son, brother or husband was serving alongside women in battle, I would be furious at the additional risks they would be subjected to if they felt any obligation at all to try to rescue women who had fool-heartedly made themselves a hazard to the male soldiers. I imagine that the military does some training to ensure that gender isn't taken into consideration when making frontline decisions, but until the testosterone is completely bred out of men, they're going to try to save women.

Yesterday's News...Confederate Monuments II

Whenever another brouhaha erupts regarding the American Civil War monuments and combatants, I have the thought that one aspect of this ongoing conflict isn't addressed.

Many of our families had men fighting on both sides of the Civil War. For some of us, that circumstance was a repeat of the Revolutionary War when we had both Patriots and Loyalists in the same family. The earlier war was divided into those who were loyal to the King of England and those who were the new American Patriots. Most of the Loyalists left for England or it's territories after they were defeated in the war, leaving behind only those who considered themselves true Americans. When the Civil War erupted 78 years later, it was between <u>Americans</u> who weren't going anywhere, win or lose.

Before the beginning of the Civil War, the westward expansion of the country was in full swing, which meant that old regional loyalties had begun to lessen for those who pioneered their way west. For those who stayed put in the South after her defeat, it would make sense that their loyalties strengthened as they came under ever more pressure to concede to the Northern viewpoint. Whether those southerners dug their heels in over slavery itself or over being told that they'd lost a war on their own land and had to do things someone else's way is debatable.

What isn't debatable is that, while many generations of Southerners, black and white alike, chose to move forward with their lives and raise happy, productive children, others opted to impose their old hatreds and resentments into their children's psyches.

Also not debatable is the fact that, even if your Confederate grandfather had been designated as a hate-filled loser by history, he was still your own kin and you felt that he had been an honorable man doing what his country asked of him. This may be as true of the southerners who have been wallowing in anger for generations as it is of those who are optimistic, productive and patriotic folks.

<u>You</u> might call your own uncle Frank a pig-headed miser, but let someone who's not family agree with you and you're going to put his lights out.

116

That's how I suspect southerners in particular, but many others who had close kin fighting for the South in the Civil War, feel when organizations come barreling in and try to take down the monuments to those soldiers. Those are monuments to people's Grandfathers, uncles, cousins and families; not just to the General who led the charge and has his name on the plaque. It's a risky proposition to tell relatives, even 150 years later, that their kin were evildoers fighting to keep slavery alive and well. Especially when most of those soldiers didn't have a slave to their name and were just doing what they saw as their duty.

For the diaspora of former southerners who have settled in Montana, Arizona or Oregon, their old family connections to that long-ago war and the people who fought it have probably dissipated. To modern day southerners who have stayed close to their roots, maybe still putting flowers on graves of seven generations of family in the same cemetery, the relationships can be much more solid.

It's this personal connection to dead family members that I feel many don't allow for in their zeal to destroy monuments to a cause that (thank goodness!) no longer exists. The cause no longer exists, but the human descendants of it, black and white, do. You want to be careful what you say about someone else's kin, no matter what they themselves may say about the old bugger.

117

Equal pay has long been a yardstick in comparing men and women in the workplace. If a woman has equal qualifications for the job and no children, then equal pay *should* be the law. But from an employer's point of view, most women are going to be less reliable workers than men while they're raising children. I realize that fathers in this era are taking on more of the tasks of child rearing and that if mom and dad are making equal money, he should be just as likely as she to take a day off here and there because the kid has chickenpox or a cold. That may happen, but, generally, I suspect that mom's going to be the one calling in. Even more likely if the couple is divorced and mom is the custodial parent. When taking an unscheduled day off throws the employer's schedule off, nobody cares because the employer isn't the one with the rights in this scenario, is she?

When I was in my 30's or 40's, I decided that I'd rather have a female Gynecologist now that there was such a thing available where I lived. I was happy with my choice until the day she decided to quit practicing medicine so she could raise her young son. She referred her patients to another woman in the practice who soon took a leave so she could move to Africa (or some such place) for a few years. In my 70+ years, I've never had experiences like that with male doctors. Sure, they move or retire once in a while, but their replacements are reliable. They don't seem as free as their women co-workers to just pick up and go off on a lark or to change their minds about career options.

Eyes will pinwheel when I say this, but we raise more well balanced children when there are two parents under the same roof. A mother and a father. And one of them should actually be parenting on a fairly full-time basis. These days, there are a lot of careers that can be conducted on flexible schedules that adapt well to child-rearing; maybe keep that in mind when choosing a major in college? Do you want to be a parent or do you want to farm out those duties so you can have a career that 'matters'? If your kids don't matter, then you shouldn't have them. Keep your knees together until you decide if you're Mother material or not and whether ten or fifteen years of parenting counts a fulfilling and challenging role for you. If not, no shame; have a great life and don't feel that you have to explain your choices to anyone.

Advice: When I hit menopause, my Mom counseled me to not start on the hormone regimen women are all (still) pushed toward. Her doctor had advised her at that stage to tough it out for a few years and she'd be through with it instead of still having hot flashes at 90 (as her friends went on to have). It worked for me. Do some research before committing yourself to years of drugs for something that's a natural process.

...17... <u>WOMEN AND RAPE</u>

My Daddy said fifty years ago that if a man rapes, he needs to be hanged.

Fifty years later *I'm* adding that if a woman lies about being raped *she* needs to be hanged.

When a woman lies about being raped she is denigrating and trivializing the valid claims of all who are <u>actual</u> victims. She is taking something akin to a misdemeanor offense and elevating it to what should be a capital crime. This offends and infuriates me. For a whole culture to have now emerged that encourages this slutty, often money-grubbing behavior shames me as a woman. Being felt up or having your butt patted does <u>*not*</u> measure up to rape. You shouldn't have to be touched if you don't want to be, so put on your Big Girl pants and handle it. And don't equate the dumb cluck who did it to a rapist.

Men who commit rape against women (or sexual touching to any degree against children of either gender) should be permanently removed from society because they will continue to be a threat; *rape* is nothing about sex and all

121

about violence even when there are no black eyes involved.

Why do women wear make-up and dress to flatter our figures? Do *not* give me that 'I do it for me' baloney. Sure, we like to look our best, but we also like to entice men (yeah, okay, *or* other women, let's do be inclusive, here). And there's absolutely nothing wrong with that! Good men will notice and give you props for it, don't bust their balls for that. Bad men will notice and do bad things, but they'd do so (and *have*) even if you were wearing a nun's habit.

There's a distinction between being raped and *any* lesser act of sexual harassment. Harassment is not 'sexual' just because it might happen to a *woman*. Bullying happens to people because they look different, belong to a different political party, dress funny, or a million other reasons. Harassment isn't right, but if you haven't yet learned some effective ways to deal with it by the time you're an adult, then you were too sheltered a child.

Rape, on the other hand, is *excruciatingly* serious. Bad men will not care how you look or what you're wearing. Rape happens when a plumber attacks a homeowner, when a woman is abducted and assaulted any number of times by any number of men, when a 'guest' sets upon a hotel housekeeper. Or, as happened to a dear family friend, when a woman in her 80's is raped and killed in her home by a snot-nosed bastard who thought he owed her one.

Whether or not a rape survivor reports the crime may depend on her age as well as whether she lives through it. Having to relive the whole thing to the cops and on through an investigation and trial may be more daunting than many women can face. If she *does* have that strength, it could help to keep a predator from injuring others, but I don't blame a woman for focusing on taking care of herself.

The rape survivor needs and deserves all help and support in her journey toward incorporating this heinous event into her psyche and in how she chooses to allocate space to it in her self-view as she moves forward. No one, woman, man or child, should ever have to travel this road.

I've known women whose own brothers molested them when they were children (I also know that including fathers, uncles, etc. and expanding beyond my own acquaintance would multiply the number immeasurably). Whether or not you choose skillet revenge in a case like this is up to you, but the women I know chose to write the miserable sons-of-bitches out of their lives and are living *excellent* lives. Those men should have been hanged; they were rapists.

I've never betrayed those or the other rape and assault confidences I've heard over the years, but I would caution young women that, if you choose to share your most mortifying experiences with friends, _they_ will never forget. They may always view you with compassion and as a winner and survivor, but they will never forget. What you want out there about your life is up to you and if you choose to put the incident away entirely, it can be unhelpful to have other people knowing about it. Confide sparingly.

I know very few women who haven't got a personal story of men behaving inappropriately with them. The worst of those men are pigs who _deserve_ an iron skillet to the back of their heads. However, if you instead decide 30 years later to seek revenge for it, I hope that your recollections haven't skewed over time and that you have impeccable witnesses because this zeal to hold people accountable for unprovable, he said/she said events that may or may not include actual rape is damaging to all concerned (except the lawyers).

Most of us have sons, brothers or husbands who, at one time or another, weren't sure where the line was drawn (and that line is different with each woman and every decade) and may have inadvertently stepped over it. Do you want to see the men you love excoriated and destroyed _now_ for a youthful indiscretion that _did not_ *include* rape? If not, try to look at it from that viewpoint before you ruin a man or encourage others to do so.

It's stupid for women to not realize that most men are (until they all get totally emasculated by MeToo) slaves to their dicks; testosterone rules. We'd all like to think that the fellows *we're* partying with are more highly evolved than that, but no. Drinking lowers the inhibitions of men and women alike, making them each think that they're the most clever, irresistible person in the room. Men think that vibe means women want sex. Women *might* mean that, but they just as often think that flirting and teasing is all the fun they're after. Men of all ages are lousy at interpreting those subtleties and, depending on how fundamentally decent they are and how well they were raised, things can go south in a hurry.

Please don't think that I'm making 'boys will be boys' excuses when all I'm doing is explaining that men and women are different. Yes, it's a shame that you can't party with men the same way you can with women, but you need to be your own best advocate.

If you've foolishly contributed to putting yourself into a drunken, highly charged sexual situation that resulted in your being raped (*raped*, not leered at, scared or felt up, for Pete's sake) you probably feel some shame and guilt along with the fury. After all, Mama *told* you not to

125

go...If a party rape has happened, it's devastating but it is also necessary for you to *own your part of it.* (Look at it this way: if you step out in front of a rolling bus because you didn't look up from your cell phone, is it on the driver that he mowed you down? You have a responsibility to be aware of your surroundings and to react accordingly.) You will recover faster emotionally if you take your share of the responsibility and don't label yourself as a victim. (I hope you were at least able to tear his nuts off before he sauntered out of the room). Your own wounds will heal if you let them. If you keep picking at a scab it just becomes a scar and, once again, that's your choice to make. Shit happens; try to learn from it and move forward.

Don't think that my attitude means that I've never experienced any of the depredations discussed in this chapter. Certainly I have. I learned my lessons, licked my wounds and never looked back.

Here's a quiz. I recently heard this story on a Phoenix radio station: A bunch of adults were at a party and one guy got so drunk and obnoxious that his friends asked him to leave; they sensibly took his keys and wouldn't let him drive home. Rather than calling Uber, some woman from the party volunteered to drive the guy home in her car. He came to enough along the way to assault her. Who's to blame?

A] The drunk B] The dumb-as-a-box-of-rocks woman C] The other partiers D] All of the above

Advice: If you'll train yourself to sleep on your back, you will have many fewer wrinkles on your face and chest than if you sleep wadded up in a ball. (plus it's actually healthier for you!) Courtesy one of the Gabor sisters & Merv Griffin; ca: 1960's.

...18...WOMEN AS VICTIMS

Women as Victims. Boy, *that's* the hashtag for the 21st century, isn't it? Because I go out of my way to avoid whiny, indignant victims, I'm aware of few of the movements claiming to empower women and feel no need to participate. I do have to comment, though.

One current scam making the rounds that I *am* aware of is the get-rich-quick #MeToo shakedown. You know how this is played, right? Some woman drinks/smokes/snorts too much, sleeps with a powerful man who she thinks might make her famous or marry her and, when neither of those happens, she cries assault and ruins his life. Pretty simple, huh?

There are variations on the claim of 'assault' ranging from inappropriate touching, comments or lecherous glances, fear of rape and actual rape. This is contributing to throngs of women (and some enlightened men...looking to score) 'supporting' each other online and in public places.

An aside...on whose dime are protesters (on any topic) while they're Twittering or swarming the courthouse steps? I've been an employer and would not be happy to be picking up the tab; but to object would just make the employer one more abuser, wouldn't it?

In the last few years, lots of men in the news, political and entertainment fields (the guy who works at the carwash isn't a very lucrative mark) have been the targets of these brave new feminist stalwarts. In an era when universities are compelled to provide Safe Places for college kids to cower from the realities of life, it's not surprising that young snowflakes have no clue how to handle workplace aggression by men except to turn the victim/make me rich/give me my 15 minutes card.

Let me *tell* you how to handle that guy: fight physically, make a loud scene so that you've got witnesses and hold the creep's feet to the fire *right then*, not 2 or 20 years later. What've you got to lose? He's already made it clear what it will take to keep your job, hasn't he?

You can't have it both ways; if you want equal pay, advancement opportunities and the chance to serve on the front lines with the men, then you'd damned well better toughen up. That doesn't mean you have to let yourself be used, it means you should fight on the turf you're given rather that making a scene where it does no good at all.

Women's shelters all over the country are full of women who are victims of some pig of a man who walked right through useless paper restraining orders to beat the hell out of her for the umpteenth time. He doesn't get locked up for long because he has 'rights.' That's what our laws have come to: protecting an abuser's *rights* rather than his *victims*. Don't equate these women with a gal who lets some sleaze talk dirty to her so she can go on camera and get famous.

Yesterday's News... Victim Mentality

Golly, is everyone else as sick and tired of the pervasive new 'victim mentality' as I am? Obviously not, or it wouldn't be dominating the media in all it's rainbow glory. But I mean those of us here in the real world.

I see that Georgetown University recently held a large, formal ceremony to apologize to the descendants of 272 slaves sold in 1838 to pay off the university's debts.

That's ugly history, no doubt about it.

Leslie Baker

A Reverend who spoke offered profound apologies for having "greatly sinned" in the sale of the slaves. Unless that fellow is pushing 200 years old, I doubt that he has much sin linked to the incident being commemorated, but he was willing to flog himself over it.

Some of the attending slave descendants magnanimously recognized the apology as a "positive step toward atonement," but noted that the "unparalleled pain still burns in the soul of every African American".

Really? How so? While I'm sorry for the circumstances of slaves (whether Roman, Mexican, Black, Irish, female, Indian, or whatever) and for the problems it brought to their IMMEDIATE descendants, I've never understood how people born more than fifty years after one atrocity or another can claim to be much aggrieved by their ancestors' suffering.

Yes, I get that the laws haven't always kept up with changing mores and that there are always bonehead bigots around the fringes, so please spare me a lecture on my insensitivity and ignorance.

There is NO ONE who couldn't find a niche for their own particular brand of 'I've been discriminated against' whine if they're of that mindset. You're Tall? Black? Gorgeous? Jewish? Tattooed? Short? Female? Ugly?

132

Mexican? Fat? Old? Disabled? Indian? Sexually undecided? Painfully ordinary? SO WHAT?! Deal with it. All of us have our trials, but few of us have a valid reason to expect society to fix them for us. Pissed off, I get; entitled, not so much.

Infinitesimal minorities of people are now responsible for the changing of laws that affect every American. Their 'rights' run roughshod over those of the rest of us, most of whom are just plugging through life with no intent of harm to anyone.

Institutionally sanctioned monstrosities have happened throughout history and continue today. This doesn't make them right or excusable, but shouldn't make them piggy banks, either.

Most of us (including those of us involved in genealogy) can cite atrocities done by or to our own families if we go back far enough.

I show quite a few slave-owners in my family tree. Nothing to be proud of but I don't harbor any guilt over things that happened in an entirely different era and long before my ability to influence anything.

In 1692, my 9th great-grandfather & -mother lost two of their daughters to hanging during the Salem witch-hunts.

Barbaric? Yes. Excusable? No. But also not something for me to wring <u>my</u> hands over. It's a curiosity in my ancestry but has zero impact on my life. Can you imagine what an idiot I'd look like if I claimed harm or sought reparations on that basis?

Now, there are plenty of people who'd tell you that I <u>absolutely</u> carry those witch genes, but don't you believe them.

Bill Cosby's accusers waited 30 some years before deciding that he had heinously abused them. Got them *their* 15 minutes of fame, didn't it? When they were stoned young star-fuckers having a go at a famous, rich Hollywood guy, I imagine that it was a pretty fine line of coke that determined who was using who. But now they're abused. Give me a break. Cosby was convicted because he was a conservative black guy who was so uppity as to lecture other blacks for some of their lousy choices. And because a couple of very savvy lawyers put out a dragnet for 'victims' to share the TV time.

At this point, few of the men who have been toppled from power by this movement have actually been tried and convicted in a court of law. Instead, they've been fired on often-meager evidence and fleeced of their money because of the insane mob mentality sweeping the country. I'm gratified to see that a few of them are quietly being given second chances in their careers. I would want the same for the men in my life. Of course, the men who are serial abusers are toads, but if women weren't willing to do damned near anything to get or keep a glamour job, some of this would dissipate.

Getting into a he said/she said in a courtroom and having a jury so amped up on misplaced MeToo righteousness that they ignore 'innocent until proven guilty' and vote for the supposed victim just because they would feel bad *if* her story could be proven should be everyone's worst fear for the state of our justice system. That's *not* a great standard to set, ladies.

Some of the powerful have *always* taken advantage of the weak and that behavioral phenomenon isn't limited to the film and political businesses. It happens in banks, bars, coffee shops, grocery stores, churches, carwashes and everything in between. It has always happened to *anyone* (not only women and children) who is vulnerable to someone in a position of relatively more power.

The single most important thing that we as women can do (and to teach our children) to keep from being susceptible to the advances of users is to *not be vulnerable*.

135

Having children you can't reasonably support without public or family assistance is the very best way I know to put a huge target on your back. And don't fool yourself that the father (husband or not) of that child is going to be any help at all in raising it. If he is, great, but _you_ are the one who must bear the responsibility for your children for the next 18 years. If you're not armed with a decent education and some skills, you will be vulnerable to every slimeball who wants to put his/her hands on you before s/he hands over that paycheck.

Please don't raise your daughters to believe that there's any reason on earth to go to a man's hotel room to chat about a script or discuss raising broccoli. There's _one_ reason to go to that room and if you're so stupid that you don't know that, then you and your mother should both be locked up.

Ladies and gentlemen, do you really want children? If not, and if you're secure in your personhood, get a tubal ligation/vasectomy. Why take the chance, every time you have sex, that your life is going to be upended by lifelong responsibilities and moral obligations that you're not interested in? For many people, children are the whole point of life and bring joy that far outweighs the pressures and aggravations involved in parenthood. But, if you're in the 'Meh' camp, save yourself (and everyone else potentially involved) some grief by cutting those cords.

For those who weren't blessed with strong, loving families to instill a sense of self-worth into their children of any gender, it's hard to overcome the lack of that most important value. The courage and good sense to be your own best advocate may not come early enough in life to save many from being their own worst enemy until they've made some colossal errors; I get that and am sorry for anyone in that position; please just *try* to not be the low man on the totem pole.

One caveat that I've not heard anyone mention in this women-as-victims uproar is that women and teen-age girls can be as treacherous in their own right as can predatory males. A teen girl (or boy) bent on rebellion, honing her skills of flirtation or manipulation can be a worse threat to a man than a Black Mamba. Many a man has had his life destroyed by some kid who may later have wished she'd not posed as eighteen years old when she wasn't, but didn't have the maturity to fess up and _he's_ living out his life as a Registered Sex Offender. Or he was an 18-year-old having sex with his high-school girlfriend and her parents had to 'show him.' Grown women can be vicious vipers and don't even have the excuse of immaturity to hide behind. Women are most certainly not *always* the victims.

Advice...Regrets are useless and damaging. If it's not too late to make something right, do so and scratch it off your list. If it is too late, put it on a shelf and don't pick at it. Be gentle with yourself.

...19...ABORTION

Many young people begin taking a meaningful interest in the larger world in their 30's and 40's. It's a heady time of raising children, building careers and noticing how the political landscape really *does* affect your life. For many, it's the first time since college that they have a 'cause' that isn't dictated by academe. They can see how the tax structure and the regulatory environment determine how much money they get to make, keep and invest. They begin deciding how many non-contributors they want to support alongside their own families. And how they want to raise their kids (they get no say in how the other kids they're supporting are raised). Many are gung-ho for their right to have an abortion since they're apparently too busy to remember to take their readily available birth control pills.

Yesterday's News...Mother's Day

Men, I hear John Deere calling your name. Unless you have a PhD in Interpreting Foreign Languages, this will not be your cuppa joe. Childless women, I hope that you, too, have a tractor (or a Maserati) waiting in the driveway. Only mothers of adult children (MAs) will relate to any of this

There is nothing so foreign to a woman who has stumbled through child rearing than to wake one day to find that her fully grown kid might as well have been raised by wolves. You look over your shoulder, mouth agape, thinking that surely to God, your progeny is standing behind and not in front of you.

But, no. No, this is indeed the apple of your eye, the fruit of your loins standing there saying something offhand that feels like a smack with a cold fish. And with no ill intent! She's not angry or upset, she's just noting that you haven't a clue how to clean the shower door that you've been cleaning beautifully every day of her life and most of yours. Or when_____. Fill in the blank quickly; with most of these slights, we mothers forget them almost instantly. I think it's a self-preservation skill given by God at conception.

This superior attitude of a young adult is not a new phenomenon. I doubt that there are any MAs who haven't raked themselves over the coals for some of the thoughtless, hurtful, careless things they're suddenly reminded of having said to their own mothers. Looking back, we realize that we were way too old (maybe even had children of our own by then) to have been such trolls to our mothers. But we were so cocky and sure that we had this nailed; we knew how to handle life so much more competently than our provincial little mothers ever had. It took some casual slight by our own kids to dredge up that cringe.

All of this comes from a woman who's been blessed with a son whose name appears in the dictionary as the definition of "perfect son." Trust me when I say that I totally realize how lucky I am! Nevertheless, a few cold-fish moments have ensued.

I guess that the bright side of this situation is that at least we MAs get those patronizing, smug, moments from our kids while those poor, childless wretches don't. Before WE die, we have some time to twist in the wind, realizing the pain that we inadvertently caused our mothers. That they tolerated our condescension, our superior forbearance of their unsophisticated ways, our eye-roll as we tsk-ed at their comfortable shoes is amazing. And, for too many of us, we've lost the opportunity to apologize; our Moms went to their graves loving us in spite of the miserable bats we sometimes were to them.

The childless among us have no one to teach them the lessons of humility that we proud MAs are taught. No, they have the option of going blithely through life secure *in the knowledge that their mothers loved them with no "in spite of...." insights to cloud the glow.*

We mothers only gain the insights by having them reflected down a hall of mirrors to us through the beautiful eyes of our children and our mothers. Any hurt we feel is forgiven almost before it's felt, on and on through the generations.

Happy Mother's Day!

I'm one of many pro-choice conservatives who feel that abortion should be legal through the first trimester, but rare. Every woman I've known who had to make the wrenching choice for abortion at some time has been dogged by it. Some feel that it really was the only viable option at that point in their lives but are still saddened by it. Others regretted it while their feet were still in the stirrups. But they *all* know how old that baby would be today. I'm grateful that it wasn't a choice I ever had to make, but I would never want to make the decision for anyone else.

Men should have <u>no</u> say in what a woman does with her body and I don't think that most of the men on the Supreme Court want to see any such case looking them in the eye. If idiot activists on *both* sides would just let things alone to perk for a few years, it could become a non-issue.

Advice: To make <u>any</u> history feel more relevant when you read it, learn your dearest grandparent's birth year. You'll always have a touchstone for when events happened in the overall timeline. Then remember another date a generation further back.

...20...GENDER

First, I can't resist noting how insanely appropriate it is that the androgynous mule is the symbol of the political party pushing the gender wars.

For the mom who's raising her small children in the new gender-neutral zeitgeist, I have some thoughts.

This is all on you. You've fallen prey to the thinking that men are toxic predators, women are victims and children are born neither male nor female but whatever they choose to be as early as they choose it.

As long as you and your family live in politically liberal, densely populated enclaves on the extreme geographical edges of our country you can probably make this mindset fly. Should you face a job transfer to somewhere in the real world, you may encounter some blowback.

Men and women are different. Or at least they used to be. In the hair-on-fire extreme left, it's no longer fashionable to recognize gender differences and certainly not to celebrate them. This rush to androgyny has begun emasculating men and turning women into a bunch of wannabe Amazons (and we're not talking shopping, here). I'm astounded to see some of the men I've known for years politely handing over their balls for society to use as doorstops holding open the portals to a gender-free world. They seem to think that standing in solidarity with Neuts (not sure what the members of this idiotic movement are called, so I empowered myself to give them a name) gives them some cred as nice guys. I think it makes them look totally whipped.

Doesn't this neutering of both genders seem a radical accommodation to the vocal minority of the other-gendered in our society? Many sources estimate that they make up fewer than 5% of the U.S. population but we in the majority have allowed the urge to be hyper-inclusive to eclipse our common sense and change the way we live. *We* have no protected rights.

Yesterday's News…A Gender-Free World

For all of us who are now identified as 'cisgender' (men or women who were born the same gender with which we 'identify') this is a confusing time. Who knew that 'male' and 'female' would become inadequate to describe us? Did you know that, in 2014, ABC News identified 58 'gender options'?

Have you read that children as young as 3 but more commonly around age 12 are being given 'cross sex hormones' to help them transition to whatever gender identity they've chosen for themselves? And their parents are all for it! You'll be shocked to hear that I'm speechless.

On that topic. I'm fully speech enabled on the subject of transgenders in the Military.

The men I know who served in the military in the 1940's-60's were wholly aware of the gays ('queers' was the word in those days and has returned to today's lexicon in ways that no one seems quite able to explain) who served beside them. Long before it became official, there was an unspoken "Don't Ask, Don't Tell" understanding among all involved. Even the DADT policy was deemed too discriminatory by Barak Obama in 2011, when he repealed it so that gay military members would no longer be "....forced to hide who they are..." At least none of this entailed do-si-do bathroom policies.

Now, I don't care if trans/bi/tri/multi-genders (you'll note that I don't even try to keep up with the ever-changing LGBTQXYZ acronym) serve in the military as long as that tiny percentage of the population doesn't demand or receive any special treatment. By that, I mean that they agree to use the bathroom and shower that matches their birth-gender, that their 'openness' doesn't become a point of conflict with their fellow troops and that my tax dollars don't go to their trans-surgery. My feeling is that you'd better plan to leave the military the same physical gender as you went in.

I am <u>SO</u> not interested in what you do or who you do it with in the bedroom or the backseat. Really. If you're a foot-fetishist, like to play dress-up or are into bondage, go for it and be happy, just leave the rest of us out of it. Is that too much to ask? I don't want to see rainbow-bannered parades with people performing sex acts while parades featuring elephants have been deemed barbaric; isn't that backwards?

By now, most of us oldsters have come to terms (if uneasy ones) with gay marriage and spouses of any gender being an accepted part of society. Many would have been happier for this to have resolved in relationships (<u>with</u> benefits, for Pete's sake) that could have been identified as something other than 'marriage,' (Fusion? Melding? Blending? Surely some word would have been lovely enough to work) leaving the term 'Marriage' for the religious, one man/one woman set; but we were too timid and politically correct to have claimed marriage as our own.

So, here we are in a world many of us don't recognize. It makes me wonder why we ever bothered to ban polygamy. If anything goes, then there are no limits, right? If your babies can make gender decisions before they can drive, drink or vote, why can't you marry your potbelly pig?

There have been gays as long as there have been people and, until recently, they've always been discriminated against. We could all find something to justify the 'victim' label for ourselves if it proved advantageous. The current enthusiasm to be all-inclusive has meant that gays and Neuts are more accepted than ever in history but it also feels like those who don't have a label to hang around their neck are the ones being discriminated against.

And I resent like hell being forced to use unisex bathrooms. Until gender neutrality reaches the level where all men are sitting down to pee, I don't want to be forced to share a john with them. Recently, on a college campus, I had to use a toilet with a urinal at my shoulder; wanna think about *that* ick factor? Do I have to get pee on the cuffs of my pants because some idiot somewhere is afraid his/her rights are being infringed on? I'm sorry, but screw that.

149

Ladies, this is all on you. Just as no sane man will interrupt a woman with her face buried in an ice cream carton, they're all going to choose battles over *anything* in this atmosphere very carefully. That includes the raising of their children.

I hope that, since you've painted your son's fingernails all his life and have now decided to send him off to his first day of 'real' school with a shiny new coat of bright red polish, you've also prepared him for the very real fact that he may get the crap stomped out of him; for the fact that not all have embraced the idea of having their gender identities stripped away. Although I feel reassured that, even though the kid's id may be permanently damaged by gender confusion, he may not get beaten up; I've been reminded that, where you live, many other children are being indoctrinated in the same manner. What a relief.

On the off chance that some child at your son's school *isn't* as evolved as you are and pummels your child for being different, I hope that you won't get your shorts in a twist and huff into the principal's office complaining of bullying. You will, of course, because you, too, are a 'victim' spending your life on the lookout for slights, but I wish you wouldn't.

You obviously drained the last of your husband's testosterone in the production of your children, since he

150

has put up no more resistance to the neutering of them than he has to his own impotency. Even the grandfathers and uncles of your children are straining toward the ideal of androgynous equality and suppress any thoughts of rebellion. You're the mom and it's *your* choice, but all of them join you in responsibility for the confused children you're raising.

Today, as I'm not even finished with this chapter, there's a story on the wire about a nine-year-old Colorado boy who had shared with his mother that he was gay. When Mom enthused over his revelation, he hurried to school to proudly announce the big news. He was then so mercilessly bullied that he killed himself. At 9 years old.

You are the parent here. Don't infer that your kids' exploration of her or her friends' genitals means she's gay. She's being a kid. Tell her that it's usually best to keep her hands to herself and don't make a big deal of it. Then, tell your husband to grow a pair and help you to raise confident, decent *men and women*. You won't let your child put her hand in a flame, cross the street alone, walk up to strange dogs; why on God's great green earth do you suppose that she's any more prepared to make decisions on her *gender*?! Jeez girl, you won't even let her use sharp scissors yet and you think she's got the wherewithal to *determine her gender!* What is the *matter* with you?

Back in the dark ages, when my son might have been exploring gender options, the poor kid was pretty much on his own; I don't remember that I or any of my friends even *thought* about discussing the topic in depth until our (grown) kids had arrived at their own decisions. We raised our girls as girls and boys as boys. I *did* give a fist pump when I discovered a Cindy Crawford poster in his closet when he was about twelve just because it indicated one less parenting hurdle for *me* to jump. Later, when he was bound and determined to date every nationality listed at the U.N, I told him repeatedly that I'd love whoever he brought home as a partner but that life would be easier for both of them if their pairing wasn't too wide of the norm. Norms do change and evolve, but they're always there; life is hard enough and no parent likes to see their children make choices that are going to make it harder.

If your boy reaches 18 or 20 years old and decides that he'd really rather be a she or partner up with another he, so what? You and all the people who matter are still going to love him and you will have given him enough of a backbone to make that decision with full knowledge of what he's choosing. Just don't take the easy way out and tell a *baby* that they get to make all the decisions that you're too wishy-washy to make. Or that you think make *you* look like a MeToo pillar.

I've mentioned the emasculating of the male population. If a man's having been coerced into raising gender neutral children hasn't done the trick, having his career destroyed because he flirted with a fellow employee or made a newly inappropriate comment ought to do it. Just the specter of lives going down in flames must make men scared to death to ask a woman out on a date, not to mention risking a first kiss. How is a man ever going to get wood if he's being more careful than a brain surgeon with his every word and move around women? When there's a potential lawsuit lurking in that bottle of wine? He's not, that's what. He's going to become a total wimp so afraid of offending the predatory women out there that he becomes unattractive to the nice ones.

There you go! Gender neutrality! I'm *so* glad to be old. When sex was still an option for me, I loved it and the men I enjoyed it with. I loved the vitality and passion involved. I would totally *not* love having to coax some poor, deer-in-the-headlights twerp into dropping trou and trying to romp.

Advice... While I'm a believer in the totally inexplicable practice of Homeopathy, please don't ever let any of these loony 'alternative medicines' convince you to skip your children's vaccinations. Just be careful about bundling them.

...21...KIDS, GUNS, MENTAL HEALTH AND EDUCATION

Forty years ago, the 'guns' and 'mental health' parts of this chapter's title would have seemed out of place. Sadly, that's not the case today. School shootings by nuts are a terrifyingly modern occurrence.

There's no way to minimize the horror of mass shootings whether at work, play or school. There *are* ways to put them in perspective. I hate statistics because you can make them say anything you want them to say, so most are suspect. If you're going to search Google to conduct your own study, I urge to go to at least page 10 to avoid Google's world-view. Page one is great if you're shopping for a lawnmower, not so much for unbiased choices on hotbed topics.

Deep breath...In round numbers:

30,000	<u>total</u> gun-related deaths per year in U.S.	
19,000	or 65%	are suicide
5,100	or 17%	are drug/gang related
1,950	or 16.5%	other, including justified police shootings
450	or 1.5%	are mass shoorings

If you take gang violence and suicide out of gun statistics, the U.S. gun homicide rate of 5,400 looks similar to other G20 countries; ie: nearly non-existent.

Separately, for comparison, 40,000 Americans die annually from drug overdose; 36,000 from the flu and 34,000 in car accidents.

And we're concerned about the *guns*?! When 2/3 of gun deaths are *suicides* who would use a car, a razor or jump off a cliff if they had to?

The gangs? Personally, I'd like to see them all penned up together with enough guns and ammo made available to them to take care of the problem themselves. But I guess that would violate their 'rights,' huh?

The 450 deaths attributed to mass shootings are committed primarily by people who should have been institutionalized a long time ago.

Logic has completely taken a powder on this topic. People, get your flu shots, keep your nose clean, don't text while driving and use some common sense instead of warm, fuzzy 'feelings' about the mental health monster in this country. Guns don't kill people any more than ATVs or jackhammers do. People who don't use or have common sense are the determining factor.

Before the 1970's, you could drive through any rural area and see shotguns or rifles in gun-racks mounted in the back windows of many of the pick-ups there. Some of those trucks and guns were owned by boys still in high school; boys who also carried pocketknives on a regular basis. The theft of those guns was almost as rare as was locking your vehicle.

I don't remember *any* kids ever being shot or stabbed in our Arizona farm town. There were probably a couple of hunting accidents, but I don't remember even those resulting in death. (I do remember one poor kid being badly maimed by being run through a huge, green cotton-picker...should we ban those?) Neither adults nor kids went on killing sprees in spite of the fact that there were always guns readily available.

This should tell anyone paying attention that it's *people*, not guns that are the problem in this equation.

Also readily available in those days were institutions (yes, I *do* realize that that's a dirty word) for the mentally challenged. We had at least two institutions within 50 miles of our farm town that housed the mentally ill of all ages.

With the advent of 'mainstreaming' of the mentally disabled and government involvement as a way to handle mental health issues, we've been blessed with literally uncountable governmental departments, committees, regulations, grants, appropriations and innumerable 501(c)(3) 'non-profit' organizations, institutes and alliances _all_ raking in and doling out our tax and charitable dollars at staggering rates. Everyone involved in this circle jerk is making money hand over fist while we have more lunatics running around than at any time in our history. The pharmaceutical companies (which still can't cure a cold, for Pete's sake) are instrumental in keeping this flim-flam going.

Have you younger people heard this old saw? The scariest nine words in the English language are: "I'm from the government and I'm here to help." Never truer than today. The government can't cure mental illness; all they can do is dole out *your* money to shysters in and out of the halls of congress with reassuring sounding titles on their letterheads.

Meanwhile, all of the crazies (from the mentally challenged to the criminally insane) with all of their *rights* are killing the rest of us, degrading our schools, defiling our public spaces and making themselves crazier. How many times have you heard reference to free clinics scattered around that are supposed to dole out some poor guy's meds to him while he pushes his shopping cart from his home in a doorway to the soup kitchen? If he's *that* insane, do you think that he has a clue when it's Clozapine Wednesday? Or between 9AM and 3PM? Don't be stupid. The poor guy doesn't know his own damn name most of the time and if we as a society were actually trying to do the right thing, he'd be housed in an institution where he'd be warm, fed, clean, safe and tended to. But, no. He and millions of others just like him are sleeping on sidewalks in their own excrement and vomit, under- or over-medicated most of the time, always in danger and often a danger to others. And we're supposed to feel evolved because we haven't 'locked him up'?! *Lock that poor devil up* and take care of him with some of those billions of dollars being pissed away in efforts to keep him 'free.'

Of course, there are plenty of 'Cuckoo's Nest' horror stories about the old mental institutions, but we would

Leslie Baker

have been better off to have used some of our zeal for
regulation to clean them up than to have virtually
eliminated them. This morning on TV, a devastated
Police Chief was trying to make sense of the latest
senseless mass shooting. Speaking to the flock of
reporters, he used the term 'mental health professionals'
more than once. Many mental health 'professionals' are
not only full of baloney, but are regulated into irrelevance
by lawmakers who have been bludgeoned into protecting
the 'rights' of every lunatic, doper and criminal out there.
At the expense of the rest of us.

Do you think that one word of what you've just read is
going to change anyone's mind? No. Because 'gun control'
like 'rights' is fired into the psyche of the left by the
ACLU and the left wing media. Just imagine if all of that
outrage and funding was poured into actually eradicating
drugs and gangs (*irrespective* of their friggin' rights) or
building mental institutions and lobbying for the repeal of
laws which have kept lunatics, gangs and drugs on the
streets for thirty years and counting.

Education's a topic that I rarely pay much attention to as
I'm old and gave up on public education a long time ago.

I've opined for years that public schools were not
designed to function as daycare centers open to even the
most disabled or unruly children. During the 70's and

80's, institutions that had been charged with the care of the developmentally disabled and/or unruly of *all* ages were closed down so that these citizens could be mainstreamed into society to 'fulfill their potential.' Concurrently, all semblance of discipline was abolished in the public schools that, along with police departments, were destined to take the brunt of the upheaval.

Mainstreaming was a utopian, hippie philosophy that has resulted in millions of poor souls living under bridges rather than being safely cared for in institutions. And in millions of beleaguered parents raising children whom they no doubt love but are reliant on society (ie: the government/us) to help raise them because it would be beyond politically incorrect to institutionalize them. And in the education system we have today.

Teachers, with no meaningful reevaluation of their situation by parents, school boards or the voting public, were suddenly expected to be caregivers, counselors and wardens to a *minority* population of students whose diverse needs simply could not be met by an educator without degrading the quality of education offered to the *majority* of the students. Especially when that over-tasked teacher had been deprived of any effective tools of discipline required to just maintain civility, much less teach.

Throwing more money at the current educational situation without looking first at the misuse of the public school system as a warehouse for children with special needs isn't the answer.

We made the difficult choice to move my son from his charming, white-picket-fence public school to a private one as he entered third grade. Because he was so intellectually precocious, I'd made the batterass decision to put him in school as early as he qualified, resulting in his being the youngest, smallest kid in his class for several years to come. (Not something that you'd guess from the handsome, dynamic 6'2" guy we see today). By second grade, his teacher had him helping other kids with their work and wanted to have him skip a grade! No. He was smart and well mannered but that didn't mean that he was socially or emotionally ready to be in with kids 2 years older than he was. Or to be acting as a teacher's aide.

The situation as it stands is unfair to all of the kids (and their parents) who hope to receive a basic founding in the STEM subjects and to learn how to learn. The majority of students, just by their normality (yes, yes...another dirty word) are terribly neglected and shortchanged by a system which tries to be all things to all children. The situation is *grossly* unfair to teachers who are not trained as and who didn't sign up for careers as mental/behavioral health practitioners and who have no methods available to them to maintain a respectful learning environment.

There's something to be said for the clarity brought by a ruler whacking your knuckles. When people my age were school kids, we certainly got disciplined for misbehavior at school and the worst anxiety brought on by it was hoping that you didn't get your butt blistered at home for the same offense.

Today, you can be arrested for smacking your kid's rear in the grocery store. So nobody does it. My son is almost 40 and I think that his generation was among the last to experience any level of discipline from parent *or* school. They were also among the first to receive trophies for 'Participation' in spelling bees and baseball games, (even if they couldn't spell their own names or find the ball) all but completely degrading the trophies handed out to the genuine winners. It began to be politically incorrect to recognize *winners* and *losers* in any area of life. Talk about setting up whole generations for unrealistic expectations! Could the inability to handle failure and criticism or being so ouch-y about everyone's 'rights' have anything to do with the degraded mental health in the country?

A funny story. When my son was in his mid-twenties, he was dating an 'older woman' who had a child of around 7.

After they broke up, he told me that the main reason was that he could not stand that the child was being raised with no restraints on her behavior; that she needed nothing more than a good butt-busting, which he, of course, was in no position to administer. Even though he'd gone through a stage of feeling that there was *no* reason to ever smack a child (ie: *him*), he'd come out the other end of that relationship with a little different perspective.

There's a difference between physical discipline and physical *abuse* of a child. Kids are like mules; sometimes you have to get their attention before you can teach them anything. They're tough and they'll be just fine but if they don't learn some lessons from their parents, life is going to hold many unpleasant surprises for them.

About the only thing that my son's father and I ever agreed on after our gawdawful divorce was that Matt's choice, halfway through college, to become a ski bum wasn't going to be financed. He had been going to school hundreds of miles away from either parent and had worked for spending money while his housing and school expenses were supported. The 'no school, no money' edict gave him a truly beneficial life lesson; he slept in his car and showered at a gym more than once. It was brutal for me to contribute no more to his well being than Subway Sandwich coupons for birthday gifts, but that was the deal. To his credit, he never asked for a plug nickel and soon realized that graduating from college was a better career path than ski bum. He's built a sterling career and is a super responsible man; I suspect that he'd agree that hard lessons are sometimes called for.

Can a teacher even raise his voice over the hubbub anymore? Parents never taught the children under his care that if the teacher (*or a cop*) says 'jump' your reply is: 'Yes sir! How high, sir?' No, the little darlings all have *rights* and even their parents don't discipline them much less allow anyone *else* to do so. Chaos doesn't benefit anyone and certainly not children or teachers.

Or cops. Possibly the only folks more adversely affected than teachers by putting all of the crazies on the street and raising children with no meaningful discipline are cops and other first responders.

I am always going to give every cop every benefit of every doubt until all the facts are in. If you want statistics on how many cops are bad cops, go to Google and find them yourself. The bad ones need punishment, just as bad doctors, teachers and preachers do, but are you going to damn them *all?*

Cops do work and put up with crap that *no one* gets paid enough to do. They do scut work that the people they're trying to protect wouldn't dirty their hands with. They're cursed and spit at and see things that most of us couldn't stomach. Every day. Every day they leave home knowing what awaits them. And yet they do it, while hoping that they and their fellow police officers get to go home that night. Alive.

These people are often the only barrier between you and catastrophe, give them the thanks and respect they deserve for trying to protect your dumb ass.

Advice: When my son was an infant, we had a delightful elderly neighbor who told me even before his first Birthday that, until he was 10 or so, we should only invite the same number of guests to his Birthday parties as his age. So, if he was turning 5, we invited 5 kids, etc. Some of the best advice I ever got! Kids can handle that size gathering without melting down. And you can host that many attending adults for a concurrent cocktail party!

...22...POLITICS

I'm old enough to remember when you could be friends and have lively discussions over food and wine with people of another political party. When the only three television networks' News programs offered up *news* and not opinions; when newspapers had an Opinion *Page* and not a political creed and when you could choose a car without it's reflecting on your gender choices. I find the world since the Internet to be a tiresome thing.

If one thing I say could be heard, it would be this:

The United States Government doesn't have one dollar of it's own.

Every person (including the millions of government employees, the blended workforce (which camouflages as 'private' workers paid with government funds) people on welfare, retired politicians and millions more) who is taking money from the local, state or federal government is taking money from *you*. You, your employer and the corporations who provide your lifestyle options are supporting them all with taxes! Government money is *your* money. Period.

When all of our taxes for a given year are insufficient to cover the government's expenses, which has been the case in 45 out of the last 50 years, (*not* coincidentally, the same time frame in which the current welfare state has blossomed) the U.S. Treasury *borrows* money to make up the difference which, of course, means that we're also paying interest on that debt. We <u>all</u> owe the national debt taken on by our government to pay for all of the programs we demand.

Every time there's an election, you decide how to spend your money, so those choices need to be for things that you're *willing* to see your own taxes (and the country's deficit) raised for, because they <u>will</u> be raised.

The vast majority of those who are taking money *from* the government (whether through Unions, welfare payments or other 'free' programs) are going to vote to keep that money flowing *to* them, and that means they'll likely vote Democrat. Why? Because as a general rule of thumb, Democrats are for *enlarging* the reach of government and Republicans are for *reducing* the reach of government. Giving people money that they haven't earned is a Democrat staple which will segue into socialism.

Keep in mind, in this era of renewed fascination with socialism, that socialist leaders do not produce or provide goods and services to their citizens when the cash flow to the top is interrupted. Since individuals in a socialist society are (theoretically) not allowed to make more than pocket-change from their efforts, the people below the upper echelon are the ones who end up killing and eating their household pets when the dictator needs another palace. The workers are basically slaves and we've already discussed how lousy an idea it is to allow yourself to become enslaved.

Now, I'm not saying that we don't need government employees and 'services', just that we don't need them in the vast quantities that we have them. Certainly we need infrastructure and medical contractors but most of these services are provided on a more cost-efficient basis by private enterprise.

Don't decide on a political party because you like their slogans or campaign ads or because your favorite media darlings tell you what to think. Decide first who *you* are; what *you* truly believe. This isn't a one-day project. Every decision you make is going to have a domino effect and impact things that you hadn't even considered.

Do you believe that each of us has the obligation to provide for our children and ourselves? *Or* do you believe that it is your job to provide for your neighbor and his children in addition to your own? This *is* an either/or question and your honest answer will help you to decide whether you're on the right or the left side of the political spectrum.

There are many on-line quizzes aimed at determining on what side of the political divide you fall, but I find most of them pretty simplistic. It takes a long time to not just know how to identify oneself politically, but to be able to be see how those beliefs play into the full range of real-life consequences. You have an obligation as an American to be either a truly *informed* voter or to take a pass on voting at all. If there's an issue on the ballot that I'm not clear on, I'm perfectly comfortable in leaving that one blank.

I always used to say that I was a fiscal conservative and a social liberal, now I'm more likely to say I'm a Republican and I resent the social climate that has painted me into a box that isn't always a good fit. I used to vote for members of different political parties on the same ballot depending on how I thought the person was going to treat my community or pet issue. With the current polarization, that's not a choice many of us are now comfortable making; we feel that we have to protect 'our' side even if some particular candidate is a perfect dolt as long as he has the desired D/R next to his name. Besides being a pathetic state of affairs, that's an even more compelling reason to choose your party carefully.

Choosing Libertarian, Green or other splinter groups on the ballot is pissing away your vote to make yourself feel that you've made a 'statement'. Even if you're a rabid gambler, you have to look at the odds and acknowledge that. It generally makes more sense to be pragmatic about *your* issue vs. the big picture.

Let's talk illegal immigration. I can't imagine that anyone is against *legal* immigration, but that isn't how the media portrays the issue. The word 'illegal' isn't even uttered in most discussions on the border crisis. We are a country of laws and we have borders. People who cross our borders *illegally* have already broken our laws before they do anything else. They overwhelm our schools, hospitals, and social services to the point where we can't begin to budget for desks and beds much less the big picture items. It is radically unfair to allow this influx of illegal aliens to keep happening when we have people waiting in line for years to enter our country *legally* and to become contributing citizens. And when we have plenty of our own citizens who need some help in life.

My husband is among the first generation of his family to be born in the U.S. His grandfather came from Mexico legally in 1910, bringing Phillip's father and 6 other children. After many years of hard work and scrimping, the children became naturalized citizens and built successful businesses and careers. Most of the men in that family (including Phillip) served in our military. That's how immigration should be done. It's also interesting to note that Phillip, like many whose families have done it the right way, is a hard-liner on illegal immigration. You wouldn't even want to guess at *his* border control policy!

Because the Democrats were so dead-set against the border security provisions in the last DACA bill to go before congress, they wouldn't pass it. I'm in favor of DACA and hated to see it go down, but it was more important to the left to have it to use as a rallying tool for their base in the next election than to get it passed. That's what our politics have come to.

Yesterday's News...Fred's Plan

The "Dreamer" approach to awarding citizenship to kids who were brought illegally to the U.S. by their parents has never garnered enough traction to be in place.

Our friend Fred, a retired military man who also worked in the juvenile justice system, has the best solution I've ever heard to the problem. It's undoubtedly way too simple and inexpensive a plan to appeal to the bureaucracy, but that's not us, is it?

Fred's idea is that ALL High School Juniors and Seniors should receive instruction that will enable them to pass the Naturalization tests given for citizenship. The kids who are already citizens will learn a lot and the ones who are not (and who maintain a clean criminal record) will have the support that they need to pass the Citizenship exam with confidence.

While participation in the courses will be mandatory, non-citizens will be assured that the legal status of their parents and other family members will remain confidential as regards any information obtained through the course.

The school district would be the signer of the Affidavit of Support for the students studying for citizenship. This sponsorship should entail no cost to either the student or the district and will last until the student attains citizenship at graduation. This is a vast simplification of the current processes (and my research on the matter was pretty limited, so don't hang me if I've got some terms or explanations botched) outlined on the DHS website that explains the Naturalization process, but it's certainly doable.

Leslie Baker

What a thrilling day it would be for the kids who graduate with not only their High School diploma, but also their United States Citizenship! And what a win for all the rest of us to have kids who can go on to college and actually be able to USE their diplomas, or to have young people who can enter the workforce legally. While it doesn't address some of the older dreamers, I still love this idea.

Another idea I love is one that my husband has held for many years. Phillip (who saw action as a gun commander during the Korean War) has always said that, upon completion of a full tour of duty, an Honorable Discharge, and completion of all background checks, anyone who serves in the U.S. Military should be awarded citizenship. I completely agree; what finer allegiance can be shown to your country than to be willing to put your life on the line for it? The people who do so shouldn't be required to jump through further hoops to qualify as citizens.

I'm a hard-liner as far as law enforcement on illegal immigration goes. Individual stories that you see or read about illegals can break your heart, but the fact is that people here illegally are breaking our laws and cheating all of the people who are going through the process legally.

174

Children who were brought here by their parents had no choice in the matter, have attended school and church here and know no other way of life. Regardless of what ultimately becomes of the whole mess, I think that we need to show some flexibility when it comes to the Dreamers.

Fred's Plan might be part of the answer.

———————

Even *with* insurance, how much did it cost you when your children were born? But if you were indigent and/or illegal, it would all be 'free.' Does that make you feel all warm and fuzzy to know you're picking up the tab for all the babies being born to illegal and indigent women? And that you'll *keep* paying for their education, medical care and the next generation of the same?

Increases in the Minimum Wage sound like such a great idea! It will help that guy flipping burgers to feed his family of four; awwww, isn't that kind and caring? Well, no, it isn't, because as soon as the owner of that business is slapped with wage hikes, he's going to cut jobs. He's running a *business*, not a soup kitchen.

And that guy flipping burgers? If he's trying to support a family in that job, he's made some poor life choices and should never have had kids. I applaud him for working rather than going on welfare, but he needs to add some vocational training (and birth control measures) to his schedule. The reason this kind of job is referred to as 'dead end' is because they're self-limiting. They were never meant to provide a living wage but as a place for high-schoolers to get a feel for what work really feels like or to give a retiree some extra cash.

These are only a couple of scenarios to consider in deciding what your political beliefs are. Until you own a business that is slammed with the massive costs of complying with every single regulatory requirement (in fields as diverse as medicine, fast-food and construction), you may not see that <u>more</u> government does not mean <u>better</u> government. Until then, it's easy to say that there should be more laws and 'protections' governing commerce, carry on about the rights of workers and scream about the greed of corporations.

My son noted a few years ago that businesses (ie: their owners) who are the *least* impacted by government regulation tend to be those who are *most* politically liberal. I have to agree that when it comes to the titans of technology and the social, entertainment and print media they've come to dominate, that theory seems to hold water. The tech fields are still so new that regulation has had a hard time catching up. The new young media giants are the richest people in the country and until they understand what unbridled government regulation means to *their* industries, they're going to be all for it for everyone *else*. That's *US!* Most of us have mortgages and car insurance to pay before we can throw a few dollars in the Salvation Army bucket, and we're going to be the ones getting taxed to death by the liberals.

Advice: My Gramma's advice is as true today as it was when she gave it and as when I shared it with my son: Don't give in to cynicism in your attitude. Irony, skepticism and sarcasm have their places, but cynicism is a soul killer.

...23...NEWS

W e're all what we read or listen to as far as our world view goes. When most of the dispensers of 'news' have become outlets for only their own *opinion*, and that opinion is mandated by the liberal tech giants who own those outlets, it verges too close to totalitarian forms of government-run media for my taste.

If you want to see something in a Google search that isn't reflective of the political leanings of Larry Page, Mark Zuckerberg and the like, you usually have to hop six or eight pages ahead and does anyone *ever* look beyond that first page? I'm pretty sure that Siri and Alexa don't, either. Ergo, you're only seeing a liberal point of view.

Yesterday's News...Sorta Health News

I'm so excited! There was an article somewhere recently positing that people who cuss like sailors tend to be more truthful than those of you who keep a civil tongue in your head.

That's just so great. For years, I've vowed to stop swearing or to at least learn some more refined expressions from either Shakespeare or early politicians. But, when exercised, all of those delightfully bawdy phrases dessert me and I'm left sounding like an ill-educated longshoreman on a bender.

But now you know; I'm at least telling the <u>truth</u>, fogged in a blue haze though it may be.

Big article in the Republic a couple of weeks ago about the possible "over-diagnosis/over-treatment" of breast cancers. The article doesn't get into whether or not the same may be true of prostate cancer screenings, but I wouldn't be surprised if that's the case. For years we've been told that regular breast and prostate exams were absolutely essential.

In the news the same week was the revelation that, if you expose your kids to peanut butter from an early age, they're much less likely to develop peanut allergies; which struck me as kind of a Duh moment. HOWEVER....is this the straight scoop or will there be a rethinking of it, too, down the road?

I don't think that many of us over 60 ever had a childhood friend with peanut allergies, and we all lived on the stuff. Now, I'm not belittling the deadly effect that a genuine peanut (or other) allergy can have on a person. And, like most families, mine has been impacted by breast and prostate cancer. I wouldn't wish any of these on any family. You have to do what you can to protect yourself and your kids and we tend to rely on 'experts' to tell us what that might be.

But the 'experts' often blow it. They come out with these grand pronouncements one year and five years later say "never mind". I quit taking them very seriously some years ago when the headline was that milk was bad for you; a few years later came the never mind on that.

How are we to know when the sky is really falling and when someone just got ahead of themselves in announcing findings? Beats me.

Swearing, health screenings, allergies; scientists have and share opinions on all manner of topics. Sure, we have to wait five years to see if they really mean it, but I'm going to look at it as a pass to cuss (truthfully!) to my heart's content for a few years more.

For years I watched both CNN and Fox News and felt that I got a pretty balanced view of what was going on in the world. While there are chowderhead loonies on the fringes of both sides of the media aisle, I now feel that I get more actual *news*, as opposed to *opinion* on Fox News. Something to remember about both CNN and FNC (forget MSNBC who knows no mode but 24/7 hysterical, hair-on-fire outrage) is that their prime-time evening programming tends to consist of opinion shows while the daytime programming (one of which, Special Report with Bret Baier, I record to watch later) tends to be news oriented. *Opinions* are like noses, everybody has one and they're a lousy way to get what you perceive of as *news*.

Let me offer a few more thoughts. For those of you who wouldn't want your friends to know you're trying to look at both sides, I promise to keep my mouth shut. Here are some programming ideas that might ease you into getting information that conveys both sides of the political story. The best place to start is (Stuart) Varney & Co. daily on FoxBusinessNews; it's a lively mix of financial and political news and a great way to see how they intersect. On FNC, Media Buzz (Howard Kurtz) is on Sundays and looks at the media coverage of the news in the previous week; again, a great mix. I'm not a fan of *anybody's* opinion programming on TV; the few minutes at the end of Special Report scratches that itch for me. I do enjoy...wait for it...Rush Limbaugh who I only hear if I happen to be driving when he's on. His bombastic style just makes me laugh while it seems to make many young people quiver in such shock and indignation that they can't hear his usually solid message. The programs I've suggested here really *are* fair and balanced.

Please broaden your news horizons and don't get everything from the links on your Facebook page.

Advice: In my teens, I suffered a serious back injury. I recovered but always just accepted that I'd have arthritis at the site when I got old. Well, I'm old and don't have arthritis, but more importantly, I've suffered remarkably few episodes of massive back pain through my life. I believe the reason is that, as a result of that early injury, I was taught at a young age how to lift properly. If you will lift with your legs and butt and <u>not</u> your back and <u>never</u> twist at the waist or hips while lifting, you'll be ahead of the game.

...24... THE UPSIDE REDUX

No kidding! There are a *lot* of upsides to being a Millennial! You have many good years ahead of you.

You can influence the science and medical fields to improve the outlook for your geriatric years. You can determine what can be done about plastics. Maybe explain to someone like me why they can't all be melted together in hotter-than-hell vats and poured into forms for use as stepping-stones or building blocks?

You still have time to raise your kids to be wonderful people. You can raise the stature of trade schools so kids aren't made to feel like morons for attending them. No matter how technology impacts them, trades such as plumber and electrician are going to have a place in society for years to come. Qualified tradesmen usually make a good living and don't carry massive student debt for 40 years. Find a way to take the stupid stigma away!

You can enter politics and leave those kids an improved world. Our country's founders never envisioned 'politics' as a career move, one that would keep you on the public dole for the rest of your life. Farmers, lawyers and mechanics were all to serve a few years and go back to their actual careers. Public service was to be a shared responsibility. You might find a way to get us back to that model.

Yes, you and your children are facing a different world than your parents faced; see what you can do with it!

I'm going to leave you with words shared with me many years ago by a good friend from Canada:

Life should not be a journey to the grave with the intention of arriving safely in a pretty and well preserved body, but rather to skid in broadside in a cloud of smoke, thoroughly used up, totally worn out, and loudly proclaiming
"Wow! What a Ride!"

— Hunter S. Thompson 1937-2005

Go for it! Your parents love and are rooting for you!

AUTHOR PROFILE

L eslie Baker is one of the most opinionated, thoughtful and intelligent old ladies writing today and she loves a spirited discussion.

Having lived most of her life in flyover country, Leslie is a little prickly at the way 'her' people are ignored by the mainstream media. She has strong opinions on MeToo, Hospice care, Gender Neutrality and damned near anything else you can name!

Born and raised in Arizona, Leslie lived a couple of years in Northern Alberta, Canada and about twenty-five years on either the Central Coast of California (where she raised her son) or in a tiny town in the foothills of the Sierra Nevada Mountains. She and her husband now live in the Arizona mountain community where she summered as a child.

For most of her working years, Leslie was involved in the real estate and construction industries. She was among the first single women in the property management field; co-owned a construction and engineering firm; held a

California Real Estate Broker's license and most enjoyed her years 'fixing and flipping' residential properties.

For over twenty-five years, Leslie has been an intermittent volunteer with Hospice organizations in the communities where she's lived. She currently has an opinion column that runs in the local newspaper.

Watch For Leslie's New Book

Old Lady Porn

A collection of short stories to take to bed at night

Available soon on Amazon

If you enjoyed Fireworks! *please* give it a quick
review on Amazon, Goodreads or
wherever you talk about your books.

Many Thanks!

ACKNOWLEDGEMENTS

My family and friends have been so patient and supportive through the writing of this book! In particular, I thank my husband, Phillip Mojica, my son, Matt Sansone my brother, Bob Baker and Mike Cremieux for their input.

The Lakeside Writer's group was a nurturing and empathetic place for a new writer to test the waters. Jacque Hamilton of Soapbox Edits offered many good editing suggestions and prodded me to establish a social media presence, which isn't going to happen, but she tried!

I thank God for His favor and blessings throughout my life.